20

Biggest

MISTAKES
Principals Make and
How to Avoid Them

Marilyn L. Grady

CORWIN PRESS
A Sage Publications Company
Thousand Oaks, California

For information:

Corwin Press
A Sage Publications Company
2455 Teller Road
Thousand Oaks, California 91320
www.corwinpress.com

Sage Publications Ltd.
1 Oliver's Yard
55 City Road
London EC1Y 1SP
United Kingdom

Sage Publications India Pvt. Ltd.
B-42, Panchsheel Enclave
Post Box 4109
New Delhi 110 017 India

Printed in the United States of America

Library of Congress Cataloging-in-Publication Data

Grady, Marilyn L.
20 biggest mistakes principals make and how to avoid them/Marilyn L. Grady.
    p. cm.
Includes bibliographical references.
ISBN 0–7619–4600–4 (cloth)—ISBN 0–7619–4601–2 (paper)
    1. School principals—Professional relationships. 2. Educational leadership.
I. Title: Twenty biggest mistakes principals make and how to avoid. II. Title.
LB2831.9.G74 2004
371.2′012—dc22

                              2003019029

04 05 06 07 10 9 8 7 6 5 4 3 2 1

Acquisitions Editor:	Robert D. Clouse
Editorial Assistant:	Jingle Vea
Production Editor:	Melanie Birdsall
Copy Editor:	Diana Breti
Typesetter:	C&M Digitals (P) Ltd.
Proofreader:	Tricia Lawrence
Cover Designer:	Michael Dubowe
Graphic Designer:	Lisa Miller

20 Biggest MISTAKES

Principals Make and How to Avoid Them

This book is dedicated to my youngest daughter, Elizabeth.

Contents

Introduction

Experience is the name everyone gives to their mistakes.

Oscar Wilde
Lady Windermere's Fan (1892)

The principal's role in the school emerged early in the nineteenth century. The increase in the number of students and teachers led to the need for a principal to coordinate the clerical aspects of the school.

The term "principal" appeared as early as 1838 in the Common School Report of Cincinnati, and Horace Mann referred to a "male principal" in his annual report of 1841 (Pierce, 1935). Historically, the position of head teacher and principal teacher preceded the development of the role of principal. The introduction of supervision of instruction as an additional administrative task led to the gradual elimination of the teaching component of the principalship. The principal in a nonteaching role became a general trend in large cities subsequent to 1860 (Grady, 1990).

The typical progression to the principal's position is from a classroom teaching position to an administrative position. In larger school districts, there may be intermediate administrative positions between teacher and principal such as assistant, associate, or vice principal; coordinator; team leader; or head teacher. In smaller districts, teachers move directly into principals' roles. Although the early principals had no specialized, formal training for their roles as principals, in the 20th and 21st centuries universities assumed responsibility for providing principal preparation programs. Accreditation organizations such as NCATE, and standards such as those promoted by the Interstate School Leaders Licensure Consortium (ISLLC), provide guidance and uniformity to these preparation programs.

Even though principals participate in preparation programs, there are many mistakes they can make. A review of the literature concerning a principal's mistakes yields few results (Bulach, Boothe, & Pickett, 1998; Bulach, Pickett, & Boothe, 1998; Davis, 1998, 2000). Focusing on mistakes may be construed as "negative" or in bad taste. The truth is, we learn from both positive and negative examples. Without acknowledging the mistakes principals make, the profession appears to exist in a perpetual fantasy land where mistakes are never made. When a principal makes a mistake he or she must hide the event, since no one else appears to make mistakes. This is an unnecessary burden for the principal. The quote "to err is human" applies to the principalship as it does to all human occupations. We strengthen the profession by providing an honest and accurate portrayal of the position. For this reason, this book is an important contribution to our understanding of the principalship. This book is a collection of mistakes principals make.

Ideally, principals could learn from the mistakes other principals have made. For principals, who are often isolated by their position, this book offers the reassurance that "I'm not the only one who makes mistakes!" The book is specifically designed for principals as a means to reflect on their personal behavior and experiences.

The mistakes described in this book reflect many years of conversations with teachers and administrators as well as my own years as a principal and a teacher. Most of the scenarios concern mistakes that a principal can and should avoid. Unfortunately, some of the mistakes are career-ending disasters for the principals. In most cases, the mistakes are common occurrences that could be remedied if the principals would examine their own practices.

There is another genre of extreme principal behaviors that Blase and Blase (2002) describe as "The Dark Side of Leadership": principal abuse of teachers. Those pathological behaviors and their effects are not the focus of this book.

The mistakes reported here are divided into the broad categories of People Skills, People, Principal, Job, Tasks, Personal Issues, and Fatal Attractions. Many of the mistakes overlap because of the nature of the principal's work.

The People Skills section highlights the mistakes from the human relations–interpersonal relations side of the principalship. These mistakes are presented first because they are the mistakes that may cause a principal to lose a job (Cohn, 1989; Davis, 1998; Martin-Lucchesi, 1990). For this reason, avoiding these mistakes should be of primary concern to a principal.

The People section includes mistakes related to working with professionals and parents. Working with adults distinguishes the work of the principalship from the teaching role. Although teachers work with parents, in the principal's role responding to parental concerns takes on greater significance. Meeting the needs of teachers is a major aspect of the principal's work because student learning is directly related to the work of the teachers. It is the principal's responsibility to develop the best teaching staff.

The Principal section includes mistakes that reflect principals' shortcomings. These include being bossy, inconsistent, or weak. The scenarios provide a mirror for the principal, an opportunity "to see yourself as others see you."

The Job section includes the mistakes that relate to the principal's position. These mistakes are grouped as endless work and time constraints—companion concerns frequently described by principals. Managing these issues are primary challenges for adult professionals.

The Task section highlights mistakes related to the work a principal must accomplish. The task areas of the principal's role formed the early foundation of principal preparation programs. Principals are expected to master each task area in order to demonstrate fitness for the principal's role. These areas continue to challenge principals. The mistakes in this section include ignoring preparation, displacing goals, avoiding decision making, change dilemmas, professional development vacuum, and failing to supervise.

The Personal Issues section discusses family and health mistakes. These mistakes affect a principal's ability to do the job or to enjoy doing the job. If these mistakes are not avoided, principals destroy their personal lives. Families disintegrate and health deteriorates.

The final section is Fatal Attractions. The mistakes in this category can be career-ending disasters. These mistakes must be avoided since they may have extremely negative consequences.

The scenarios in each section illustrate the mistakes that can occur in each area. The spirit of the book is that principals are not destined to make these mistakes. By considering these scenarios and the discussion and suggestions that follow, principals should be able to steer clear of many of these mistakes. The principalship is an applied field, one learned through practice. These scenarios describe the practical experiences of both principals and teachers. For new principals and experienced principals, they suggest strategies for avoiding some of the mistakes other principals have made.

The mistakes reflect the real world of the principalship. Individuals preparing for the principalship and those who are principals should find comfort in knowing "they are not alone" in their experiences.

Acknowledgments

To the school administrators—Peggy Croy, Jean Haar, Barbara Marchese, Ramona Miller, and Kaye Peery—who generously gave their time to review drafts of the manuscript, I give special thanks. "Friends are like diamonds, precious but rare . . ." I am fortunate to have these individuals as friends.

The scenarios described in this book reflect many years of conversations with teachers and administrators. I am grateful for the wisdom these individuals have shared. Their real-world experiences have influenced my teaching, writing, and thinking about principals and schools.

Phyllis Hasse has polished my words on her computer for 16 years. Although I hope she enjoys her retirement, she will be sorely missed!

Cindy DeRyke has provided great assistance in the preparation of this manuscript. Her efforts are truly appreciated.

Robb Clouse has provided great advice and assistance in the preparation of this book. His attention to the "important" issues is greatly appreciated.

Corwin Press gratefully acknowledges the contributions of the following people:

Ronald G. Joekel
Executive Director Emeritus
Phi Delta Kappa International
Professor, University of Nebraska, Lincoln

Barbara Marchese
Principal
St. Philip Neri School
Omaha, NE

Barry Stark
Principal
Norris Middle School
Firth, NE

Kaye L. Peery
Superintendent
Maxwell Municipal Schools
Maxwell, NM

Karen Hayden
Principal
Brandon Elementary School
Brandon, SD

Lydia Haynes
Principal
Jim Hill High School
Jackson, MS

Dorothy T. Terry
Principal
Bailey Magnet High School
Jackson, MS

About the Author

 **Marilyn L. Grady, PhD**, is Professor of Educational Administration at the University of Nebraska—Lincoln. She is the author or coauthor of 14 books. Her research areas include leadership, the principalship, and superintendent-board relations. She has more than 150 publications to her credit.

She is the editor of the *Journal of Women in Educational Leadership*. Her editorial board service has included: *Educational Administration Quarterly, The Rural Educator, The Journal of At-Risk Issues, The Journal of School Leadership, Advancing Women in Leadership On-Line Journal*, and *The Journal for a Just and Caring Education*. She is the recipient of the Stanley Brzezinski Research Award and UNL's award for Outstanding Contributions to the Status of Women.

Dr. Grady coordinates an annual conference on women in educational leadership that attracts national attendance and is in its 17th year. She has served on the executive board of the National Council of Professors of Educational Administration, the Center for the Study of Small/Rural Schools, and PDK Chapter 15. She is a member of the American Educational Research Association, the International Academy of Educational Leaders, the National Rural Education Association, the National Council of Professors of Educational Administration, Phi Delta Kappa, and the Horace Mann League.

She has been an administrator in K–12 schools as well as at the college and university levels. She received her BA in history from Saint Mary's College, Notre Dame, Indiana, and her PhD in educational administration with a specialty in leadership from The Ohio State University.

The People Skills

Always do right. This will gratify some people, and astonish the rest.

Mark Twain
To the *Young People's Society*
Greenpoint Presbyterian Church,
Brooklyn (February 16, 1901)

The principal's work does not fit into handy compartments. In fact, there are significant overlaps in the many aspects of the job. The principalship is about working with people. To effectively work with the many individuals associated with a school, the principal must demonstrate highly refined people skills.

Principals describe the people skills—interpersonal relations and communication skills—as most important to their work and their success. The people skills provide the means to accomplish the extensive array of tasks that are the principal's responsibility. For this reason, mistakes related to people skills are presented first. The mistakes are followed by a discussion and suggestions for avoiding them.

Mistake 1
Interpersonal Shortcomings

Skilled principals recognize their importance to the positive culture of a school. They understand that greeting teachers, recognizing the efforts of all, and treating everyone equitably are standards in their interpersonal skills repertoire.

The school is people. Without a network of positive relationships, the work of the school cannot be accomplished. It is through the principal's leadership and interpersonal skills that excellent schools are created.

Scenario 1: Forgetting to Say Hello

Teachers reported that the principal does not visit classrooms except during appraisal years. They noted that they do not see the principal in the halls, and they wonder if she cares what is going on in the classrooms. They report frustration because she does not meet or consult with them. Their point of view does not seem to matter. They said, "She could at least make a point of saying 'Hello.'"

Rχ: Successful principals excel in the fine art of meeting and greeting people. A first step for this principal is to approach the teachers and staff members, acknowledge the oversight, and apologize for it (Blanchard & McBride, 2003). This action will demonstrate the principal's care, concern, and honesty. It will demonstrate her leadership.

A daily routine of greeting the teachers and support staff is essential to prevent the problem described here. The interpersonal aspects of the job have to come first.

In schools where enrollment is high and administrators are few, it may be difficult for principals to be in all the places they should. Often teachers are ignored. Those who are ignored may be the most experienced or the most competent teachers. The principal assumes that they are doing fine and that they do not need assistance. The truth is that even the best and the brightest teachers want to be acknowledged. Being overlooked is possibly an implicit compliment, but teachers do not perceive it that way. Instead, teachers who describe not being acknowledged may be uncertain about the principal's care. The principal must greet staff members daily and recognize staff accomplishments. There is no substitute for treating each staff member as a valued member of the school. Only the principal can create this culture of care in a school.

Caring leadership builds a learning community that includes everyone involved with a school. Caring affects, and some say determines, the degree of learning in schools (Barth, 1990; Caine & Caine, 1991, 1997; Damasio, 1994; Elias et al., 1997; Greenspan, 1997; Jensen, 1998; LeDoux, 1996; Sergiovanni, 1994; Sylwester, 1995) (as cited in Lyman, 2000).

The following list of common practices of caring leadership represents how principals at all levels have led schools to become more caring communities:

1. Articulating values that support caring.

   a. Caring is important in and of itself.
   b. All persons deserve to be treated with respect and dignity.
   c. High expectations for learning and achievement are essential.
   d. Treat students as you would your own children.

2. Embracing and viewing positively the complexity of difficult situations.

3. Bringing conflict to the surface for constructive handling.

4. Creating participatory approaches to decision making and problem solving.

5. Acknowledging and valuing the reality of diversity.

6. Being flexible in interpreting and enforcing rules and policies.

7. Restructuring to support caring and create community.

8. Inviting partnership with parents in the education of their children.

9. Modeling caring in culturally meaningful ways.

10. Demonstrating commitment over time. (Lyman, 2000, p. 139)

Principals must plan and schedule their days so that they achieve their goals. There are many distractions in a school day. A principal without a plan will find that days seem to evaporate with little to show for hours of effort.

Leaders make plans, establish goals, and are persistent in their commitment to achieving those goals (Grady & LeSourd, 1990). Leaders can account for their time and can document their accomplishments. "Leaders . . . are 'outer-directed.' They go toward potential followers, cultivate them, satisfy their needs. They show a 'healthy' openness to others' concerns; they give up their own project's schedule to accommodate others' demands" (Wills, 1994, p. 161).

Teachers need to be recognized and appreciated. When a principal ignores the teachers, they are cut off from meaningful contact with the key decision maker in the school. The teachers' voice is silenced. Issues, concerns, problems, challenges, innovation, creativity, and excitement are all suppressed. The interactions about teaching and learning are lost. Teachers' professional growth and development is thwarted. The ultimate "loser" will be the students. As the teachers are diminished by this principal's mistake, they will lose their enthusiasm for their work with students.

Principals should strive to create an enthusiastic teaching force that is recognized and rewarded for its accomplishments. Principals need to stimulate discussions about teaching and learning so that all the staff's focus is on their most important work in the school. Synergy is the ideal in the school setting. By forging relationships with all the individuals involved in teaching, the knowledge of all the professionals is brought to the discussion.

Scenario 2: The Cold Fish

The principal never recognized the work of teachers. The teachers said they never heard any praise for their work with students or for their personal accomplishments. Teachers received special awards and recognition, and the principal did not acknowledge them. She does not pay attention to all the good people and all the good things that happen in the school.

The principal has shown no interest in getting to know the staff. She has not taken an interest in getting to know what the teachers are doing. It is the same for the students, parents, and community. She makes no effort to connect with them. When the bell rings, she is gone. This makes communication really difficult. She does not live in the community. Her lack of interest and involvement is apparent.

Rx: Principals are often amazed when they discover how important they are to teachers. The principal's attention is a source of satisfaction for teachers. Although one may assume that teachers, as adult professionals, should be able to experience their own self-actualization on the job, in fact teachers look to the principal-leader for direction and support.

Principals should keep in mind the basics of *The Greatest Management Principle in the World:*

1. The things that get rewarded get done.

2. If you aren't getting the results you want, ask the magic question: "What's being rewarded?" (LeBoeuf, 1985, p. 7)

Recognizing the accomplishments of teachers has benefits for the entire school. Frequent celebrations and recognitions create a climate of accomplishment and progress. According to Conradt (2001),

> The simple lesson to be learned from the whale trainers is to *overcelebrate.* Make a big deal out of the good and little stuff that we want consistently. Second, *undercriticize.* People know when they screw up. What they need is help. If we undercriticize, punish, and discipline less than is expected, people will not forget the event and usually will not repeat it. (p. 93)

Student, teacher, and school accomplishments should be heralded by the principal. By these leadership actions, a principal can transform the climate of a school. By verbalizing and demonstrating what they believe, and by sharing their passion for providing a positive learning experience for students, principals shape their schools' cultures (Haar 2002a; 2002b).

Celebrating accomplishments and rewarding those who merit notice are part of the leadership challenge described by Kouzes and Posner (2002). The work of the principal often focuses on problems and crises and the "good stuff" is neglected. Principals are overwhelmed by constant telephone calls and people who "drop by" with questions and concerns. Entire days can be consumed in responding to these issues.

The principal's role is to let staff members know how well they are doing their jobs. "Effective school leaders give plenty of timely positive feedback. They give negative feedback privately without anger or personal attack, and they accept criticism without becoming defensive" (Irmsher, 1996, p. 1).

The principal needs to adopt a practice of setting aside time each day to recognize individual accomplishments. "The number one motivator of people is feedback on results . . . Feedback is the Breakfast of Champions" (Blanchard & Johnson, 1983, p. 67). Writing congratulatory notes or personally complimenting individuals only takes a few minutes. Recognizing accomplishments must be a planned part of each day. If it is left to chance, it will not happen. Principals who focus on establishing a positive school culture make recognizing and celebrating individual accomplishments a priority.

This unfortunate scenario may characterize a principal who has only a short-term interest in this position. Individuals who take positions knowing that they will be short term may not be motivated to get to know the faculty and students. This is a mistake because the teachers and students are the core of the school.

This principal's behavior may be the result of her perceptions of her role. "Isolation comes with increasing power or prestige. This can breed arrogance, as truth and sharing suffer when others are not willing to speak up to us or to correct our errors" (Carter, 1996, p. 96). Perhaps this principal has an inflated sense of her power and prestige.

The principal's job is not a "9 to 5" position. The principal's day does not end when the students leave. The principal is the principal 24 hours a day.

The teachers in this scenario clearly identify the principal's deficits. The teachers know that in a school "we feel differently about enthusiastic, growth-oriented, cheerful individuals. We gravitate to them, enjoy their company, and try to emulate them. These natural leaders share six characteristics: They know themselves, like themselves, take control, demonstrate flexibility, accept reality, and live fully" (Krupp, 1994, p. 27). Each school should have this type of individual as principal. Fortunately, many schools do.

The principal is a very visible member of a community. In some communities, the principal is one of the highest paid community members. The community expects to have access to the principal. They, in fact, may behave as though they "own the principal." Community members want contact with the principal. When the principal does not live in the community, community members may resent the principal's absence.

Principals who live in communities other than where their schools are located sacrifice a major link to the individuals they serve. Community support of the school and the school's activities is essential for success. The extra time that principals invest in being available for conversations with the public is time well spent.

Scenario 3: Playing Favorites

The principal grants special privileges to some teachers and not to others. Some teachers are allowed to leave school during the day on a regular basis—others are never allowed to leave.

The principal plays favorites all the time. She's constantly visiting with her special friends, laughing and having a grand time. Other teachers who are not her "favorites" are ignored.

Rχ: "The most important single ingredient in the formula of success is knowing how to get along with people." (Theodore Roosevelt, cited in Maxwell, 1999, p. 103). "Playing favorites," which is suggested in this scenario, is a major mistake. No one benefits from a principal's inequitable treatment of teachers, students, or parents. The principal's fickleness makes the school environment unpredictable and uncomfortable. Even those who benefit from favoritism recognize the inequities.

Most principals recognize that they must be paragons of equity in a school. All the teachers and support staff seek the attention of the principal and there is no room for favoritism. Favoritism isolates individuals and divides the faculty and staff into the "haves" and "have nots"—those who have the principal's attention and those who do not have the principal's attention. Instead, the principal should be working to establish a strong sense of community and ownership of the school's program. Cliques and factions do not contribute to a positive school culture.

Principals who build their friendship networks at school with students, faculty, and teachers often tie themselves to personal relationships that thwart their ability to make sound professional decisions. Students, teachers, and parents are not the principal's peers. The principal is bound with the teachers, students, and parents by a series of authority relationships. The principal is, first and foremost, the school leader. Personal relationships or favoritism should not be the basis for the principal's decisions. Principals should focus on Eskelin's (2001) "Reminders for Leaders Who Love (Ten Valuable Keys)":

- Realize that strong relationships are primary.
- Learn to truly "understand" others.
- Relationships begin at home.
- Build alliances based on principles.
- Set an example that backs up your words.
- Create an "open door" environment.
- Demonstrate personal and professional courtesy.
- Realize that change requires connection.
- Never betray a confidence.
- Stay connected—no matter what! (pp. 126–127)

Scenario 4: The Invisible Woman

The teachers described the principal as "public relations ignorant." They said she does not want to get out there in the public eye. She is not prominent at athletic events or concerts. She is almost invisible. They noted that she does not sponsor community meetings or the monthly coffees to visit with the community. She has not built a working relationship with the local newspaper. Even though the teachers provide information about special activities and student accomplishments, the principal does nothing with it.

Rχ: Building relationships with the school community takes careful planning and persistence. National demographics indicate that only a small percentage of a community has children in school; yet, the school is supported by the entire community. When the community has little opportunity for involvement or discussion about the school, then strong community support for the school cannot be expected. In times of scarce resources, school funding can decline when principals have failed to build community ownership of schools.

> If parents do not know about a school's problems, they cannot contribute their considerable energy and resources— their power—to resolving them. At the same time, trust must be developed between parents and educators to reduce the likelihood of each blaming the other for the problems. (Giles, 1998, p. 2)

The principal must arrange community meetings and discussions. These opportunities must occur regularly so that the principal has current and accurate information about community issues and concerns. Resource A suggests opportunities for building visibility in the community.

Remember, the principal represents the school to the community and is the first point of contact with the school. "Shared information not only can provide parents with insights regarding ways of helping their children, but also can provide school personnel with ideas to help parents to help their children" (Drake & Roe, 2003, p. 68).

The principal's job extends beyond the typical "9 to 5" workday. Supervision of activities and presence at an endless array of events are essential and expected roles for a principal. The principal is responsible for supervision at certain after-school events; and more importantly, the principal's presence at these events is an important public relations function. The opportunities these activities provide to build strong relationships with students, teachers, and parents are extremely valuable. Extracurricular activities provide access to a wide array of individuals who are concerned about the school. The principal should use these opportunities to meet people and promote the positive image of the school. Much can be accomplished during brief visits with the public.

Attendance at extracurricular events demonstrates interest and support for these school activities. People notice if the principal attends basketball games but does not attend school plays. Different parents and community members have different interests. The principal needs the opportunity to meet as many people as possible at a variety of events.

Newspaper coverage benefits the students and the school. Making the students' and the school's accomplishments known to the public helps to build a strong, positive perception of the school. "Nothing is more important to parents than their child, and they take pride in seeing their child's name in print" (Hines, 1993, p. 46). When resources are scarce, community perceptions will shape the discussions about school funding.

Parents and community members take pride in the accomplishments of the school and the students. The principal is the chief purveyor of the positive news from the school. If the principal lacks the time to attend to this important task, the responsibility for providing information to the local media should be delegated. The school and the community suffer when the school's activities are not part of the good news.

Mistake 2
Communication Flaws

Communication skills include those that are verbal, nonverbal, aural, and written. Successful principals strive to use these skills consistently and to further develop them whenever possible. Through these skills, "what matters" is made known to all.

The difference between principals who are leaders and those who are not is often linked to their communication skills. Leaders know how to communicate their goals. Only by making the goals known to all can principals expect to achieve those goals. Clear communication is the key.

Scenario 5: Open the Door

When the principal is here, his door is usually closed. We have no access to him. Maybe he has things to do, but teachers only have a few minutes each day to visit with the principal.

Rx: Many principals make a habit of greeting teachers every day. By establishing a routine, the staff can count on having access to the principal during specific times. Before school starts, during passing periods, at lunch time, or immediately after school may be the ideal times for the principal to be visible and available. Resource B provides a verbal skill self-assessment.

Principals should vary the times or class periods when they are gone. If the principal always goes to lunch at the same time, then teachers who have preparation periods during that time may never be able to meet with the principal. An undercurrent of discontent can develop when teachers sense that they do not have access to the principal.

A weekly schedule that lists staff and administrator meetings would help reduce the concerns about the principal's absences. The schedule would document that the principal is not absent but attending a meeting.

Principals should monitor their absences to ensure that activities extraneous to the school's program do not take precedence over the school. The principal should be attentive to "false" messages that may be given to the public when the principal is absent from the building, since the principal's absence may be perceived as a lack of attention to the school.

Excessive absences may suggest that a principal does not take the work of the school seriously. A negative example to the faculty may create a culture where attendance and punctuality are perceived as unimportant. The victims will be the students who rely on the teachers' and the principal's attention.

This scenario poses one of the many "Achilles' heels" of the principalship. A principal could be at school 24 hours a day and people would still complain.

Teachers need to have access to the principal. The secretary is a key resource in communicating with people who want to see the principal. A secretary who is skilled in interpersonal relations can reduce the frustration of individuals who find the principal unavailable. The principal and the secretary can reduce the frustration of the faculty by letting the teachers know when out-of-the-building meetings occur.

Teacher frustration should be kept to a minimum since it can contaminate a positive school culture. Being aware of teachers' perceptions of the school should be one of the principal's goals. Often, minor adjustments in practices can reduce the concerns described in this scenario.

The Principal Access Self-Assessment (see Resource C) provides an opportunity to reflect on personal behavior and practices. Based on the results of the assessment, goals for improvement can be specified.

Scenario 6: Secretary Snicker

> *The principal could not write a logical sentence. His spelling was atrocious, his grammar was worse. He would write letters to the parents that made him look illiterate. The secretary never corrected them. She thought the principal was a jerk and she was not interested in helping him.*

Rχ: Poor spelling and grammar skills can be compensated for by the assistance of competent professionals or the computer software that is available. The first challenge for the principal is recognizing that he has a writing problem.

As the principal enlists assistance with the problem, Duggan's (1997) "10 Steps to Effective Written Communication" should be used to guide the communication process:

1. Communicate with regularity.

2. Use correct spelling and grammar . . . proofread all communications before they are sent home.

3. Consider the audience . . . be careful not to condescend.

4. Stay positive . . . take time to compose a calm, rational letter.

5. Be direct . . . set apart important information in a list format to ensure the best result.

6. Always make and keep a copy . . . duplicates can be worth their weight in copy paper when documentation is needed on a growing behavior problem.

7. Keep it brief.

8. Use humor when appropriate.

9. Communicate partnership.

10. Don't hide behind a letter. Nothing replaces face-to-face communication. Letters are time effective because they reach a large group of people with a small amount of time invested, or they address subjects that don't require an in-person meeting at the moment. (pp. 4–6)

Extra attention should be given to the proofreading step. A qualified, trustworthy person will be needed to assist with this task.

The principal also needs to address the issue of loyalty with the secretary. The secretary described in this scenario does not appear to want to work with the principal. The principal must confront the secretary, discuss the secretary's behavior, and resolve the difficulty.

Referent power depends on personal loyalty to the principal, a loyalty that grows over a relatively long period of time. The development of loyalty to a principal is a social exchange process that is improved when the principal demonstrates concern, trust, and affection for faculty and staff. Such acceptance and confidence promote good will and identification with the principal that in turn creates strong loyalty and commitment (Hoy & Miskel, 2000). The principal must work to create a school culture that is recognizable by the loyalty and commitment that are displayed throughout the school.

Scenario 7: Fear of Groups

The teachers said the principal was threatened in group meetings. He cannot dominate or control the discussions. His solution is to simply not have meetings. He may talk to faculty members one-to-one, but we never are given the chance to hear each other's points of view. We feel isolated because of his inability to work with a group.

Rχ: Successful principals know that full communication is best. All parties need to speak and be heard, as well as to hear the perspectives of their colleagues. When full communication occurs, all perspectives are heard and the decisions that are reached and the understandings that emerge reflect synergy (See Figure 1.1).

Individuals who lack competence or confidence may be very uneasy when full communication occurs. Their reluctance to allow the free exchange of information deprives the faculty of the knowledge that resides in the school. The process of isolating faculty and consulting with them privately fragments the faculty, contributes to a climate of misinformation, and creates an information vacuum. Figure 1.2 illustrates the isolation and limits to communication that occur when the principal does not encourage the dynamic conversation illustrated in Figure 1.1.

By isolating the teachers from one another, the principal may be attempting to maintain power or control over the group. This behavior does not strengthen the school, the teachers, or the instruction that occurs in the school.

If the principal fails to build a strong, cohesive group that is capable of communicating about the school's program, then

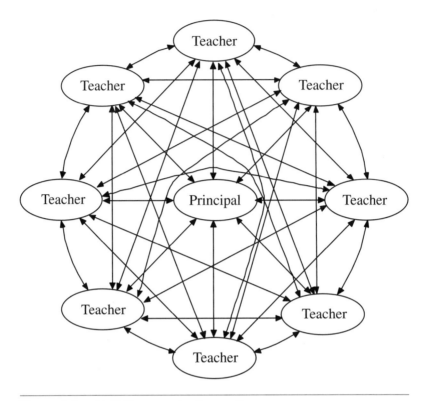

Figure 1.1   Full Communication ⇒ Synergy

the goals of the school become unclear to the teachers. Goal displacement occurs. "Faculty may become so rule-oriented that they forget that the rules and regulations are means to achieve goals, *not* ends in themselves" (Hoy & Miskel, 2000, p. 107). Ambiguity prevails. Little is accomplished. Teachers resent the enforced isolation caused by a principal's unwillingness, inability, or fear of drawing a group together.

Scenario 8: Strong Undercurrent

Many of the teachers in the building have worked together for their entire careers. Certain groups of these teachers are pretty powerful. The principal does not pay enough attention to the groups. He does not listen to their concerns. The undercurrent against him is pretty strong.

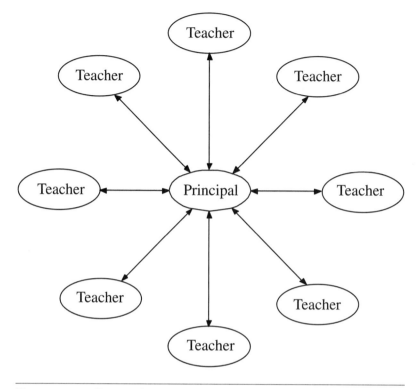

Figure 1.2   One-to-One Communication ⇒ Isolation

Rχ: "Ignorance is bliss" is not a good school philosophy. By failing to acknowledge teacher groups and their strengths and concerns, the principal is abdicating authority. The principal needs to build strong relationships with the teachers to accomplish the work of the school. If the principal does not build support within the faculty, the principal's directives and initiatives will be passively ignored. The principal's authority will be undermined.

The culture of a school is a vibrant dynamic. It is a system of informal rules that spells out how people are to behave most of the time. A strong culture enables people to feel better about what they do, so they are more likely to work harder (Deal & Kennedy, 1982).

A principal such as this one, who is figuratively "sleeping on the job," should beware. Negative teacher attitudes against the principal divert attention from the central goals of teaching and learning. The students' needs should be the most important concerns of the teachers and the principal.

The principal needs to engage with the teachers. Regular meetings should be held during which teachers' perspectives are explored.

The principal should be vigilant so that Charan's (2002) "Dialogue Killers" do not drain the teachers' energies during the meetings. The "Dialogue Killers" follow:

- *Dangling Dialogue.* Confusion prevails. The meeting ends without a clear next step.
- *Information Clogs.* Failure to get all the relevant information into the open. An important fact or opinion comes to light after a decision has been reached, which reopens the decision.
- *Piecemeal Perspectives.* People stick to narrow views and self-interests and fail to acknowledge that others have valid interests.
- *Free for All.* By failing to direct the flow of discussion, the principal allows negative behaviors to flourish.

Teachers should be surveyed concerning their impressions of the students' progress and the school's needs so that collaborative planning can occur. The principal and the teachers need to be involved in ongoing discussions about the school.

A community of teachers and learners must be reinforced with a strong dose of *social capital:* the necessary goodwill and trust to bond the community in a dedicated effort to improve the school's performance (Driscoll & Kerchner, 1999). When the collaboration requires creativity, informal gatherings where collaborators sit together and discuss the problem tend to be more productive than formal meetings (Mintzberg, Jorgensen, Dougherty, & Westley, 1996).

Scenario 9: Listen

The principal was skilled at speaking to groups: groups of teachers, groups of parents, groups of students. Her biggest mistake was that she never listened to these groups. She avoided meeting with parents. She organized meetings with teachers, but never let them speak. She did not put herself in a position where students could talk to her. She created a climate of animosity by only "giving" information and never "receiving" information.

Rχ: Anyone who talks more than she listens may be making a big mistake. Good communication is a two-way process (see Figure 1.3). Teachers and staff members are the repositories of professional know-how about teaching and learning. Parents provide information about their children and their expectations for the school. Students bring their hopes, dreams, and interests to the school. A principal who fails to listen to these voices has a shallow understanding of the students and their needs.

A principal who does not listen to teachers, parents, and students will encounter many difficulties. Decisions will not be based on good information. Teachers will begin to work around the principal. Parents will become disgruntled and find other outlets for their comments. The principal's authority will be eroded.

Arthur Schlesinger described Franklin Delano Roosevelt as a consummate networker. "The first task of an executive, as Roosevelt saw it, was to guarantee himself an effective flow of information and ideas" (Deal & Kennedy, 1982, p. 87). A principal, too, must be a consummate networker. A principal should develop open communication so that all of the constituents have a voice in the school.

As a means of self-assessment, principals should respond to the following questions.

1. Do I share accurate information?

2. Do I provide information in a timely manner?

3. Do I share information on a regular basis?

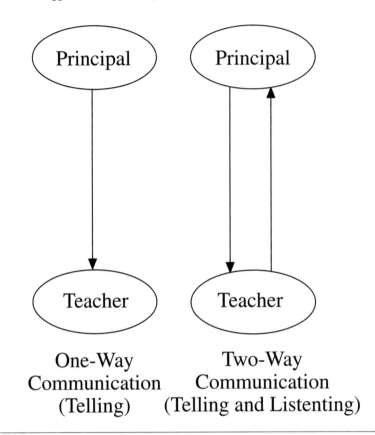

Figure 1.3   One-Way Versus Two-Way Communication

4. Am I receptive to new ideas?

5. Do I ask others for their opinion and ideas?

6. Am I accessible?

7. Have I created an effective formal communication process?

8. Do I effectively use the informal communication channels? (Weller & Weller, 2000).

In a letter to a newly appointed principal, Skelly (1996) cautioned, "Almost everyone considers themselves a good listener, and almost nobody is as good as they think" (p. 92). All should heed this caution.

The People

If you once forfeit the confidence of your fellow citizens, you can never regain their respect and esteem. It is true that you may fool all of the people some of the time; you can even fool some of the people all the time; but you can't fool all of the people all the time.

Abraham Lincoln
To a caller at the White House

The principal's work is defined by a steady stream of interactions with a wide array of people. Teachers, staff, parents, students, and community members are among the many audiences a principal meets and greets on a daily basis. As a teacher, an individual develops skills for working with students. As a principal, an individual develops skills for working with adults. The people skills identified in Part I are also reflected in Part II.

The mistakes described involve the principal's work with professionals and parents. These examples are followed by a discussion and suggestions for enhancing a principal's ability to successfully work with adults.

Mistake 3
Neglecting the Professionals

People are the greatest resources of an organization. The teachers and staff of a school bring a tremendous amount of expertise to their work. Successful principals recognize this talent and enlist it in achieving the goals of the school.

Savvy principals encourage the work of teachers. Beginning teachers as well as experienced teachers rely on the principal for support, guidance, and consistent bonhomie.

Scenario 10: Abandoned

The teachers described their experiences as first-year teachers. They said that the principal seemed friendly when they were interviewed and hired, but after that, they were left on their own. They said they felt abandoned and that they needed more support than they were given as first-year teachers.

Rχ: To first-year teachers, the principal is the most important person in the building—their "first friend." Although principals might be overwhelmed by too many students, too many challenges, and too many tasks, first-year teachers cannot be abandoned. The "no news is good news" approach is unacceptable. First-year teachers are often afraid to broach their concerns with the principal. They wait for the principal to initiate the conversation. When the principal fails to regularly visit with the new teachers, their concerns, problems, or distress may be compounded.

New teachers look to the principal for leadership. Even when mentoring programs exist, first-year teachers seek the principal's support, encouragement, and counsel. "Knowing that the principal decides whether their contracts should be renewed, beginning teachers seek some sign from the principal that they are measuring up to expectations. Most remain uneasy and fearful until they receive feedback and affirmation from their principal" (Brock & Grady, 2001, p. 41).

Principals need to have a plan for working with first-year teachers since they bear responsibility for initiating teachers into the teaching profession (Brock & Grady, 2001). The plan should include (a) activities for the time after the teacher is hired but before the orientation occurs, (b) the orientation, (c) the assignment of a mentor and scheduled mentor–new teacher activities, (d) social events throughout the school year to integrate the new teachers into the school environment, and (e) monthly meetings for all new teachers.

If new teachers are not supported, they leave the profession. Teacher talent that is not nurtured is lost. Therefore principals must not only hire the best teachers, they must nurture them so that they become master teachers. The new materials that are available to enhance classroom instruction should be made available to teachers.

When teachers leave, student learning is disrupted. Time and money are wasted when new teachers have to be hired annually. The hiring cycle, which consumes professional time and is expensive, must be repeated.

Principals need to serve as the conduit of the arsenal of instructional wealth. Students suffer if they are not provided with the best instruction available. The fault lies with the principal.

Scenario 11: We're Forgotten

The teachers described the situation for tenured teachers at the school. They said they wanted the principal to conduct formal evaluations of the teaching staff. It had been four years since the principal had been in some teachers' rooms for evaluations. For

other teachers, it had been even longer. They reported not getting
any classroom support and said they could use some encourage-
ment or tips on how to improve their teaching.

Rχ: Teacher isolation is a major dilemma in education. The
more competent the teacher, the less attention the teacher
receives. After many years of abandonment, teachers become
burned out. Their dissatisfaction with the lack of attention
contributes to their dissatisfaction with the profession. Adult
interactions keep teachers vital.

The principal must consider how much time and attention
is given to each teacher. The principal should heed Blanchard
and Johnson's (1983) reminder: "Take a minute to look into
the faces of those we manage—they are our most important
resources" (p. 8). Experienced teachers should not be
neglected. All principals report having "too much to do." Yet
principals can choose their focus. A focus on teachers leads to
the best result in a school, since student learning is directly
linked to teacher performance, and teacher performance is a
reflection of a principal's work.

A principal works directly with teachers rather than with
students. The principal's influence on students is through the
teachers. Working with teachers means working with adults.
Frequently some of the teachers are older than the principal.

Building a working relationship with the teachers requires
constant communication. It takes time and patience to develop
the communication between the teachers and the principal.
Teachers want their opinions and their goals to be known.
Only by listening can the principal acquire this information.

Principals who are leaders view their schools as communities. They recognize that communities and their occupants
flourish in caring, nurturing environments. These principals
utilize a caring ethic to guide their decisions and their actions,
and they are individuals who share vital creative, caring relationships with others (Beck & Murphy, 1993).

Trust is essential to accomplishing school goals. Trust is
built on the knowledge of others—their goals, expectations,
and behaviors. To build trust, individuals must spend time

together. The principal must plan time to build trust, develop effective communication, and establish a working relationship with each teacher.

Assuming that experienced teachers do not need administrative support is a big mistake. The best teachers become burned out when they have too much responsibility and too little support. Years of administrative neglect take their toll on experienced teachers (Brock & Grady, 2000).

A regular cycle for teacher appraisal should exist in the school. Untenured and tenured teachers should be evaluated according to this schedule. The principal needs to adhere to the cycle.

A principal should help teachers to assess themselves. Since teachers are professionals, they should decide what is to be taught and how, as they respond to the standards for their field. The principal's task is to assist the teachers in establishing a process for this self-assessment.

Indications of a teacher's successes can be found in student course evaluations, test results, or student successes indicated by portfolios of their work or evidence found in their grades. Trend data could be examined to determine progress. These data provide teachers with evidence of both strengths and weaknesses.

Weber (1995) described the principal as a mirror-maker. Opportunities for self-assessment are furthered when teachers ask themselves:

1. What will students accomplish by the end of the school year and how will this accomplishment be measured?

2. What will students accomplish by the end of today and how will this accomplishment be measured?

3. What is the difference between an A, B, and C student in terms of their accomplishment in your class?

4. How much time do you talk during a class? How much time do students talk during your class?

5. What evidence do you have that students are improving? (Weber, 1995)

Scenario 12: One Piece of the Puzzle

> *The principal acted as though he was expert at everything. He insisted on giving answers to questions he knew nothing about. He always had to have an answer for everything. He acted as though he had a better understanding of the students than the teachers did.*

R℟: Even with superb peripheral vision, a principal can only see a small part of the school. It takes everyone in the school to provide a complete understanding of the school and the students. A principal needs to utilize all the information available in a school.

Principals are not expected to know everything. Principals are expected to be able to ask questions and gather the information that is needed to serve all the students. According to Andrew Carnegie, "No man will make a great leader who wants to do it all himself or get all the credit for doing it" (Maxwell, 1999, p. 118).

A school is a knowing network. In a "knowing network, organizational competence typically resides in the relationships, norms, memories, habits, and collective skills of a network of people" (Wilkins, 1989, p. 41). The principal is only one part of the network.

The principal's role is a generalist role, not a specialist role. The skilled principal becomes expert at taking in information, asking questions, and then searching for answers.

The principal's office should not be the "Band-Aid dispensary" for problems. When issues come to the principal's attention, they should be issues of importance. Quick fixes and instant answers are not appropriate for significant issues.

All the professional talent in a school needs to be used. Each teacher has years of experience and years of education. This expertise should be reflected in the school. Principals who ignore this talent are wasting a tremendous resource.

Mistake 4
Mismanaging Parents

Mistakes principals make when they do not respond to parental requests are presented in this section. Although a principal may be inclined to delay returning a telephone call, these examples serve as reminders of the importance of acknowledging parental concerns.

Scenario 13: Jump, Jump

> *A big mistake a principal made was not jumping when a parent called. The principal reported the mess that was created when parents called the district office with their concerns. A small issue became a major issue because of this mistake.*

Rχ: When parents call, they are calling about the most important people in their lives—their children. Although the principal's day is hectic, parent calls demand immediate responses. The principal needs to listen to the parents' concerns. Not all issues can be resolved immediately, but they can be acknowledged. The lines of communication between parents and the principal must be open and nurtured.

Principals who are overwhelmed by their jobs may perceive telephone calls from parents as "just one more burden." Parent calls are exceptionally important because parents want to help their children. Parents are great resources in resolving issues children may have.

When parents call, principals need to view the parents as part of the solution, not as part of the problem. The ideal is for the principal and parents to work together to meet student needs.

"Nobody knows the child like the parent." Wise principals and teachers understand this and seek to tap the wealth of information parents have. The students' interests, hobbies, likes and dislikes, worries and fears all represent valuable information that parents should be asked to share with principals and teachers (Enoch, 1995).

The two most important things to people are their kids and their taxes, and public school is the place they both meet (Freedman, 1990). This must be understood and remembered by all educators.

Working with parents, communicating with parents, and keeping them well informed are important administrative tasks. As issues of student safety take on increasing significance, these tasks become more critical to the smooth-functioning school. Fagan (2001) noted that there is no place like school. School has become the social agency for some families. Respect, responsibility, and resiliency should distinguish a school environment that is caring and supportive.

Parents should be the first to have news of their children. Parents should never receive information about their children from neighbors, friends, or other children.

Principals need to have a plan for emergency situations. Making certain that parents are called should be a primary step in the emergency plan. If the principal needs to delegate the calling, then a secretary or another member of the staff should be designated as the person responsible for making the call.

The effective principal will spend more time working with parents and encouraging their participation in the schooling of their children. This collaboration is a hallmark of positive parent-school relations.

Scenario 14: Active Parents

The principal came to the new school from a low-income school where parent involvement was very limited. Because of this, she had not had any experience working with parents and parent groups. She did not understand the important role the parents play in the school. The parents are mostly well-educated and actively involved in the school. She is not used to this type of involvement. There have been occasions when she has not responded to parental requests. When the parents did not get her attention, they became very vocal about their disapproval.

Rχ: Some principals work in settings where they cannot get any parents to come to school, while other principals have more parent involvement than they know how to organize. At some schools, all the parents work during the day and as a result, their school involvement is minimal. At other schools, parents who are not employed have more time to be involved in the schooling of their children. Before assuming a principalship, the principal should know what type of parent involvement to expect.

Principals should pay attention to the social ecology of a school and its neighborhood . . . most schools attempt to engage individual parents without considering how differences in education, income, social networks, and positions of power can affect their ability or willingness to participate. The result is that parents from working and lower class groups are less likely to become involved in school-related activities. (Giles, 1998, p.1)

Principals need to understand the school community, the parents and the students. Many urban families will not come to the school, or will come only when summoned about their children's problems. There are many reasons for this—conflicting work schedules, low interest or lack of experience in group activities and meetings, shyness or fear about school-based activities, negative personal experiences with schooling, and barriers of language and culture. (Heleen, 1992, p. 7)

Working with parents is an important part of the principal's job. Parents have expectations for the school and those expectations must be acknowledged. More educated parents may be more adept at getting answers to their questions.

Principals who are slow to respond to parents may find that the parent communication network is alive and well. Parents who are unhappy can spread their unhappiness throughout an entire school community.

Watkins (1993) presented five strategies for working with angry parents:

1. Demonstrate confidence

2. Establish ground rules

3. Keep focused

4. Ask questions

5. Buy a little time

In a study of the conflicts principals encounter, Zalman and Bryant (2002) reported that conflict with parents could be grouped into eight categories:

1. *Principal's Inaccurate Assumptions.* This included such behaviors as should have told parents more information, and should have let mother explain why she was calling.

2. *One-Sided Decision-Making.* This included such behaviors as acted too much in an authoritarian manner, took too strong of a stand with parents, should have accessed outside services earlier, and started conversation with sarcasm.

3. *Emotional Reaction.* This included such behaviors as hung up on parent phone call, raised voice, and voice quivered.

4. *Did Not Set Guidelines.* This included such behaviors as should have ended meeting/set parameters.

5. *Unsuitable Meeting.* This included such behaviors as should have met with parent rather than called, and should have had everyone meet together.

6. *Inappropriate Location.* This included such behaviors as talked to student in the hall, not in the office.

7. *Principal Did Not Listen.* This included such behaviors as should have listened more to student.

8. *Principal's Ineffective Use of Time.* This included such behaviors as let the conflict continue on for too long, sat and listened too long, and took phone call during lunch duty. (pp. 14–15)

Principals need to have clear information before they respond to parental concerns. Guidelines for meetings need to be established. The location of meetings makes a difference in the outcomes. The timing of a meeting matters and the duration of a meeting should be planned. A principal's ability to listen, calmly and carefully, may determine the outcome of a meeting with parents.

Principals must respond to parents promptly. The Parent-Teacher Association is extremely important. Principals need to understand the history of parent volunteer activities in the school and become involved in the activities. To overcome the social gaffes described in this scenario, the principal should arrange to visit with parents and small groups in order to understand their concerns and to build stronger relationships with the parents.

The Principal

There are two ways of spreading light: to be the candle or the mirror that reflects it.

Edith Wharton
Vesalius in Zante

E ffective schools research (Grady et al., 1989) notes the central role of the principal in providing leadership for the school. One indicator of the principal's leadership is the principal's behavior. The principal is a role model for teachers, staff, and students who is expected to display the finest behavior at all times. Occasionally principals display behaviors that do not represent the finest model of leadership. When this occurs, the principal may not be aware of this behavior. The examples that follow present principals who have made mistakes by acting like "bosses," being inconsistent, and not having a firm plan for behavior management. These examples are followed by a discussion and suggestions for addressing the issues.

Mistake 5
Being Too Bossy

One of the mistakes a principal could make is assuming the posture of "the boss." This approach conjures images of the industrial model, with the schools as factory and the principal as a boss supervising an assembly line. Education does not resemble industry and the teaching and learning process does not lend itself to the assembly-line metaphor.

Scenario 15: It's My Way or the Highway

> *The principal came to the school after being principal somewhere else for 18 years. His attitude was "I'm in charge here. I'm in control. Listen to me." He was only interested in his way of doing things. He radiated an aura of "I have all the answers." He never would acknowledge that there were different ways of doing things.*
>
> *In his first year in the building, he made it very clear that anyone who did not agree with him should just move to another building. At the end of the first year, 39 teachers left the middle school. For those who did not leave, the experience was awful, because the principal's "my way or the highway" attitude was so demoralizing. Many teachers wished they had left after the first year. The school climate was very negative.*

R℈: Wise principals remember that each principalship is a whole new job. This principal's 18 years of experience "somewhere else" were simply 18 years of experience in a different job. Finkelstein (2003) cites the habit of stubbornly sticking to what "worked in the past" as a cause for executive failure.

A new principalship comes with all new people and all new challenges. One of the compelling reasons for taking a new principalship is to accept the challenge of meeting new people and new situations.

When starting a new principalship, one must enter the new position with a willingness to listen and learn. All members of the staff should be welcomed by the principal and given the opportunity to describe their goals and expectations for their work in the school. Each school has a history, culture, and traditions. It is the principal's job to learn about these. Schools are also rich social networks. Principals must identify and work with these networks. The burden of creating a positive school culture rests with the principal.

"Know-it-alls" crush creativity and participation. They allow no room for discussion or different opinions. In time, a principal will be abandoned by the teachers if there is no opportunity for meaningful discussion. A principal who has "all the answers" closes all avenues to communication.

> Here's the image of executive competence that we've been taught to admire for decades: a dynamic leader, making a dozen decisions a minute, dealing with many crises simultaneously, and taking only seconds to size up situations that have stumped everyone else for days.
>
> The problem with this picture is that it's a fraud. Leaders who are invariably crisp and decisive tend to settle issues so quickly that they have no opportunity to grasp the ramifications. Worse, because these leaders need to feel that they have all the answers, they have no way to learn *new* answers. (Finklestein, 2003, p. 87)

Principals need to find a way to "see themselves in a mirror." In this situation, the mass exodus of teachers signifies more than just teachers who moved or retired. A large turnover in staff is disruptive to learning and disruptive to students. Teachers who are left behind question their decision to stay and lament the loss of their colleagues.

A principal should document teacher turnover to determine if there are losses in staff for reasons other than moving or retirement. Staff losses should be examined to identify the extent of the principal's role in the turnover. The high turnover described in this case suggests that the principal's attitude was the cause of the departures.

The principal in this scenario has created a negative, demoralizing school environment. Instead, the principal should emphasize facilitative leadership and collaboration. A principal needs the participation of all the teachers to achieve the goals of the school. This principal needs to develop skill in working with all professionals, especially those who may have different points of view. Building unity and focusing on collective purposes should be the hallmarks of a principal's leadership.

Scenario 16: Beware the Sophist Principal

The principal walked around the school telling everyone what to do and how to do it. No one would have been surprised if he carried a clipboard and had a pencil behind his ear. He belonged in a factory. He was very arrogant. It might have been okay if he knew what he was talking about. But, if you listened to him, you could tell that he was really out of touch with kids and teaching.

Rχ: Arrogance is not a desirable quality in a principal. People want engaging leaders as principals.

Teachers are adult professionals. They do not need to be told how to do everything. Teachers have years of experience and great knowledge of their teaching craft.

The behavior displayed by this principal demonstrates a clear similarity to an ancient model that has long been out of fashion and fortunately is not prevalent in schools. The Greeks, with the lasting reputation as intellectual cheaters, were foreign experts who flocked to Athens and bore the title "Sophist," meaning "expert," with a possible sneer to it suggesting "know-it-all" (Wills, 1994). This principal fits the "Sophist" title.

The principalship is probably more of a listening job than a talking job. Competence is valued; arrogance is abhorred. Teachers will ignore or dismiss the remarks of an arrogant principal. Since teachers have critical craft knowledge about teaching, principals would be wise to respect teachers' expertise and nurture it.

A school does not fit a factory or an industrial model of organization. Successful principals focus on kind words, encouragement and listening. As a maxim, a principal should remember that "a kind word is never thrown away" (Sir Arthur Helps, as cited in Maggio, 1990, p. 8). The leader's role is to develop the leadership potential of others. This is an activity that principals engage in daily. Bennis and Nanus (1997) conducted a study of 90 leaders and from their study identified these leadership qualities:

1. The leaders had the vision or the ability to create a focus. All 90 leaders had an agenda and a great concern with outcome.

2. The leaders had the ability to translate and communicate that vision to the other members of the organization.

3. The leaders were able to establish trust through positioning. Trust is the lubrication that makes it possible for an organization to function effectively, and positioning is the set of actions necessary to implement the vision of the leader.

4. The leaders had positive self-regard and the Wallenda factor. Self-regard is concerned with a leader's feeling of personal competence, while the Wallenda factor refers to Karl Wallenda (who was virtually destined to fail when he poured all his energies into not failing rather than into concentrating on performing the tightrope walking). Leaders do not think in terms of falling or failing. (p. 32)

Principals should focus on developing these leadership qualities.

Former U.S. President Jimmy Carter described his leadership learnings with the following example. According to Carter, Admiral Hyman Rickover, the father of nuclear power, was intensely demanding of everyone who worked for him. Anything short of perfection brought severe castigation, but there was never any comment when Rickover could find no fault with the work (Carter, 1996).

Interpersonal skills are essential in education. This principal's approach resembles Admiral Rickover's. He does not know either the students or the teachers, and he does not demonstrate the basic skills required of an educator. He is confused about the role of the principal.

The principal's role, however, is not "telling" but facilitating and supporting the instructional efforts of the teachers. The majority of the principal's day should be focused on student learning (Haar, 2001b).

Principals need to establish trust with the individuals in the school. Trust is built on long-term relationships and consistent patterns of behavior. Rapport is developed through regular interactions with the staff.

Individuals want to work in an environment where the goals and expectations are clear to all. Principals provide direction in meeting those goals and the principal's presence should be the unifying force in a school. Wills (1994) offers the most important reminder.

> We have long lists of the leader's requisites—he or she needs determination, focus, a clear goal, a sense of priorities, and so on. We easily forget the first and all-encompassing need. The leader most needs followers. (p. 13)

Principals, like teachers, need to continue to grow professionally. The principalship can be isolating. This principal needs to take a fresh look at students, teaching, and learning. Professional development activities can revitalize and contemporize principals.

Scenario 17: Treat Adults as Adults

The principal was at the school for seven years. She liked being the boss. Things had to go her way. She treated the faculty like they were her kids.

She never acknowledged the fact that the teachers were adult professionals. The teachers had no voice in anything, never discussed anything, and were always told how things were going to be.

The school was in a poor, run down part of town. Perhaps she thought the teachers were losers. No one was sad when she left the school.

Rχ: Moving from the classroom to the principalship is the typical career progression in education. In preparing to make this career move, individuals often fail to adjust their working style. In a classroom, one works with children or teenagers. In the principalship, one works with adults. Different techniques are needed to work with these different age groups. Individuals who have been skilled classroom teachers may inappropriately apply their classroom management strategies in their roles as principals working with adults. Without feedback from teachers about their performance, principals can persist in inappropriate practices. This principal persisted in treating the faculty as children for seven years. This mistake was undoubtedly unintentional, and simply based on a lack of information about her performance. If a regular principal evaluation had been conducted, this principal would have been made aware of her inappropriate approach to working with adults.

The best resources any principal has are the adult professionals in the school. Each teacher brings years of experience and years of education to the job. Teachers possess a wealth of information about what is best for kids. Educator's knowledge, skill, and commitment to teaching and learning should be respected and used (Haar, 2001c).

The principal's task is to unleash the talent within the staff and enlist that talent in meeting the students' needs. The most important resources are human. Students, teachers, staff, and parents are the essence of a school. It is presumptuous to think that any principal alone would have more knowledge about what's best for students than the collective faculty would. In fact, most individuals have very few years of teaching experience before they become principals.

Teachers are adults and they are professionals. Every faculty is different and the principal must adjust to meet the needs of the group. Principals should view themselves as working *with* the faculty to accomplish school goals.

Marriott (2001) reported that it is the concrete, daily behaviors of the school leader that communicate what is valued and important in a school. Principals of effective schools continually model the value they place on accomplished teaching and powerful learning by observing classrooms; conferring with teachers, students, and families about curriculum and instruction; and by acting on policy decisions that support the school's short- and long-term goals. Effective leaders carefully and consistently model interpersonal behaviors that lead to a shared sense of care and concern.

A principal damages a school culture by being dogmatic. Self-directed teachers will lose their initiative if a principal is too prescriptive. Instead, the principal's behavior should be guided by the following example.

By giving me independence he got me to do his will. That is the way leadership works, reciprocally engaging two wills, one leading (often in disguised ways), the other following (often while resisting). Leadership is always a struggle, often a feud. (Wills, 1994, p. 11)

Scenario 18: Slash and Burn

The teachers described their principal who came to the school fresh from a university graduate program. She was full of enthusiasm and ideas. The problem was, she wanted too much too quickly. She was like a steamroller in her persistence in getting a new schedule in place. The teachers were not supportive of the idea. Her timeline was too drastic. Fortunately, she left at the end of her second year at the school.

Rχ: Schools have traditions and are bureaucracies that have their own inertia regardless of who the principal is. Teachers and staff members are part of a school culture that says "this is the way we do things here." New principals must learn the traditions and culture of the school. A level of respect and professionalism must be developed.

The principal in this scenario needs to build support and commitment to putting the new schedule in place. Without the teachers' support, the principal's efforts are destined to fail. Any change requires careful planning. Resistance to change is a natural occurrence in an organization. Change is perceived as a threat to security and can cause discomfort. In a change process, there are individuals who could be arrayed along a continuum that ranges from "innovators" to "laggards" (Rogers, 1995). All of the individuals involved in a proposed change need to have repeated opportunities for discussion. Concerns need to be expressed and considered before the implementation begins. Ownership and support for a proposed change must be established before the implementation begins, or there can be no expectation of success.

This principal's inexperience and lack of preparation for entering a new environment is evident in this scenario. Her rapid turnover as principal is disruptive to the school.

New principals need to prepare for entering a school. They need to develop a foundation for change and innovation. Because this principal did not lay a foundation for change, her "enthusiasm and ideas" were wasted.

Scenario 19: Out of the Loop

Teachers remarked about how decisions were made at the school. They reported not being invited to participate in decision making.

They pointed out that they should be involved in curriculum discussions since those decisions affect every part of their work. They said their expertise was not sought and they felt like their talent was wasted. The principal just made the decisions and passed the word along to the teachers. The teachers were excluded from a critical part of their work.

Rχ: Decision making can be a touchy issue. Some teachers are annoyed and burdened when asked to participate because they see decision making as an imposition on their time. Other teachers are offended when they are not invited to discuss every issue that concerns the school.

Teachers report being overwhelmed by what is expected of them. The changing demographics of society have changed the work of teachers. Students come to school with many needs, and teachers are expected to address those needs. Parents are often unavailable to the teachers for consultation and support. The "traditional" family no longer exists. Teachers must accomplish their work with little expectation of assistance from the home.

Expectations for improved student performance continue to drive the work of teachers. Coupled with these issues are the constant curricular initiatives that purport to improve student achievement. Teachers report being inundated by the constant introduction of new curricula.

When teachers are not involved in the discussions and decisions that lead to the introduction of new curricula, then teacher frustration is exacerbated. Implementing the curricula is the work of the teacher. If teachers do not participate in the selections and decisions then there can be no expectation that the curriculum will be properly implemented. A very negative work environment is created when teachers perceive that they are being barred from the decisions that most affect their work lives.

By involving teachers in decision making, a principal creates faculty unity, improves morale, builds support, and improves the quality of decisions. Faculty members, however, must perceive that their participation is worthwhile and that their contributions and perspectives will influence the decisions that emerge. When teachers feel their time is wasted on trivial matters, they will resent involvement (Blase & Kirby, 2000). "Some teachers do not necessarily want to take on leadership roles beyond their classrooms. They may resist because of personal time commitments, lack of confidence, or fear of the unknown" (Giba, 1998, p. 52).

Principals must find the path to being both efficient and effective in decision making. Teachers only want to be invited to discussions of topics that are directly related to their teaching responsibilities, especially those concerned with curriculum and instruction. Principals should "take the pulse of the teachers" to determine their interests in decision making.

Mistake 6
Inconsistency

Teachers highlight the mistake principals make when they are inconsistent. Inconsistencies are detected when principals do not support school policies in a uniform manner, or do not support teachers who are attempting to follow and enforce school policies.

Scenario 20: Pick It and Stick With It

Teachers lamented the principal's handling of discipline. They reported spending a lot of time developing the school's discipline policy. Everyone was involved in the discussions. However, when they tried to discipline students based on the policy, the principal did not back them up. There was no effort to enforce the policy. In fact, when the principal was directly involved, there were really inconsistent results. The same infractions were dealt with differently. Students received different consequences for the same misbehavior. Or worse yet, one student would receive punishment and another student would not. The inconsistencies created an uneasy feeling among the faculty and students. Things became very unpredictable.

Rχ: In this scenario, the teachers report the demoralizing effect of the principal's capricious behavior. In the future, teachers may be hesitant to enforce school policies due to the principal's inconsistent support.

School policy should guide decision making. Communication about school policies should be clear and consistent. It is imperative that everyone in the school understand and accept the school policies. Chaos will prevail if individuals are permitted to ignore or change policy to fit their beliefs.

Margaret Mead offered the following analysis: "What people say, what people do, and what they say they do are entirely different things" (Maxwell, 1999, p. 51). Effective schools depend on consistent enforcement of school policies. Students, teachers, parents, and administrators suffer when expectations are not clear. Effective schools have clearly-defined policies and procedures that can be found in handbooks that are distributed to and discussed with students, parents, and faculty. Principals who fail to follow the policies and procedures disrupt the smooth functioning of the school (Grady et al., 1989).

Student misbehavior escalates when students realize that all students are not treated equitably. Parents become quite vocal when students receive different punishments for identical behaviors.

This principal must enforce policies consistently and equitably in order to restore order in the school. Teachers and students expect the principal to maintain school order, and the school policies provide the blueprint for that order.

Consistency is synonymous with strong leadership. Teachers and students expect principals to behave consistently. Blase and Kirby (2000) report that principal support in discipline matters results in feelings of confidence, security, and control.

Principals must "buy in" to school policies. If a principal detects an aspect of a policy that needs revision, then the principal should go through the established process for initiating policy changes.

Scenario 21: Both Sides of Your Mouth

The new principal got himself into a snarl as soon as he started the job. His fatal flaw was talking out of both sides of his mouth. He would tell one person one thing and another person something totally different. It did not take the teachers any time at all to figure this out.

Rχ: Clear communication, consistency, and integrity are essential qualities for a school leader. This principal is creating a situation where nothing that he says will be taken seriously.

The message that a principal delivers to the faculty must be clear and consistent. A school is a large communication web. Inconsistencies in what a principal says are immediately detected. Teachers talk and rely on each other for continuous bulletins about what is happening in the school. A principal would be foolish to ignore this sophisticated communication network.

Tatum (1995) presented a list of ethical values and principles derived from the work of Michael Josephson of the Josephson Institute for the Advancement of Ethics:

1. Honesty

2. Integrity

3. Promise-keeping

4. Fidelity

5. Fairness

6. Caring

7. Respect

8. Citizenship

9. Excellence

10. Accountability

11. Protection of the public trust

Tatum (1995) suggested that contemplating these ethical values and principles could lead to another word or phrase that has a broader meaning. He chose the word "trust," a word that describes the results of actions conforming to all of the listed values. He calls the word an "icon" because it encompasses the full spectrum of ethical values. Prefacing each decision with questions such as "Will this build trust?" "Will it build long-term trust?" "How will it destroy trust?" (p. 312) would be a means of strengthening a principal's leadership and building a positive school climate.

In the studies by Kouzes and Posner (2002), their consistent finding was that the most valued quality in a leader was integrity. A principal who gives different answers to the same question posed by different people is not displaying integrity. "For the organization and its leaders, loyalty to employees means being honest and trusting, treating people as individuals and not as numbers, responding appropriately to special needs, providing resources, and, most important, acting with integrity" (Autry, 2001, p. 164). Once an individual's lack of integrity is detected, it is unlikely that that individual will be able to secure the trust of the faculty.

Faith is the foundation of organizational character. This most essential ingredient of corporate character is the "social capital." Like financial capital, social capital can be created, spent, and used up. "It is much more difficult to recapture trust, or 'social capital' once it is lost, than it is to develop it in the first place" (Wilkins, 1989, p. 25).

Mistake 7
Displaying Weakness

Principals who do not have well-developed skills in managing student behaviors may be described as weak or simply not "principal material." An example of the mistake an individual makes by not having a clear plan for student behavior is illustrated in this scenario.

Scenario 22: No Backbone—But Nice

Teachers described their reluctance to send kids to the office. They noted that there would always be a line of kids waiting for their turn with the principal. The line frequently included the same kids.

The principal was kind, gentle, soft-spoken, considerate, and thoughtful. Although the students liked him, they did not respond to his direction.

The teachers said he was weak. Although the teachers liked the principal, they said they did not get the support they needed from him.

Over time, the students' behavior got worse as they realized that there would be no consequences for misbehavior. It was a relief when he left the school for another position.

Rχ: Teachers rely on the principal for support. When students are sent to the office, they expect behavioral issues to be resolved. In this instance, the principal is not meeting the teachers' expectations.

The role of the principal requires skill in behavior management. The "enforcer" role the principal must assume demands clarity about school rules, decisiveness, initiative, and the willingness to be the "bad guy" or "bad girl" who says "No!" Meek and mild individuals, such as the person described in this scenario, may not function well in the enforcer role.

Two words that emerge in discussions about school discipline are order and respect. These are key ingredients in maintaining discipline.

Students with discipline problems generally represent a small percentage, maybe 5–10%, of a school population

(Grady, Bendezú, & Brock, 1996). Documenting which students are having difficulties and the classes in which they are having difficulties is the principal's job.

Two problems may exist. First, specific teachers may be having repeated difficulties with the same student. Second, students may not be having their needs met in the classroom. When they are sent to the office, students may enjoy the relief from the stress of the classroom. These students may thrive on the attention they receive in the principal's office.

It is the principal's responsibility to monitor the frequency of students' visits to the office and the times when they occur. Only when these data are available can the principal determine whether the teacher needs assistance with behavior management skills, or whether individual students require more specialized attention. By addressing these issues, the principal's work with students should become more effective.

Weak administrators contribute to the increase in behavior problems that often foreshadow school violence. What would have been larcenies in a well-ordered school become robberies when school authorities are not in control.

A school in which students wander the halls during times when they are supposed to be in class, where candy wrappers and empty soft drink cans have been discarded in the corridors, and where graffiti can be seen on most walls, invites students to test further and further the limits of acceptable behavior. Students get the impression that the perpetrators of violent behavior will not be detected or, if detected, will not be punished.

Principals must exhibit a strong presence, establish rapport with students, take quick, decisive action in response to situations, and administer justice equitably if school is to be a safe place. The best way to preserve a safe learning atmosphere is to have policies and procedures for dealing with problems before they occur. These include crisis intervention programs, gang task forces, police liaisons, and other programs that stay one step ahead of potential trouble. A school's responsibility to provide a safe setting where teaching and learning occurs means that reasonable precautions must be taken regarding the safety of staff as well as that of students (Grady, 1995).

In administration, there are individuals who hold line positions and individuals who hold staff positions. The principalship is a line position. A line position requires constant contact and supervision of others. The individual described in this scenario probably is not suited for a line position in a school.

Staff positions require individuals who are stimulated by working on projects until they are completed. Although individuals in staff positions work with others, the work is not usually in a supervisory capacity. The work is more often associated with a specific task. There are great contributions made by individuals in these educational roles. Perhaps the individual in this scenario would find more satisfaction working in a staff position.

Scenario 23: Zigzag Master

The teachers all tried to help him. They would listen very attentively to what the principal said. However, as soon as they tried to follow through on what he said, he would say something entirely different. When he was challenged on this practice, he would ignore the comments. After a while, the principal's inability to stick with a course of action became apparent. He may have been trying to avoid conflict, or maybe he just could not deliver on a plan of action.

Rχ: Haye's (2001) adage, "When things need to happen, you either have the nerve to act or you don't" (p. 340), applies to this principal. The principal is displaying this weakness by his lack of follow-through and the differing messages he delivers to the teachers. How can the teachers "follow" when there is no one leading?

Peurifoy (1999) lists three styles of conflict management:

1. Nonassertive = Avoid conflict

2. Assertive = Resolve conflict in a mutually satisfying manner

3. Aggressive = Win (p. 149)

This principal has adopted the nonassertive approach to conflict management. By zigzagging from one path to another he effectively dodges conflict. He cannot be held accountable for any actions since none are taken.

Individuals who avoid conflict also avoid decisions and they avoid action. No goals can be accomplished in a school if decisions are not made and actions are not taken. The school will be in a steady state of "waiting" not "doing." The issues in schools and the needs of children demand decisive action.

Bulach, Boothe, and Pickett (1998) described "should nots" for school principals. One of these was avoiding conflict. Principals avoid conflict by "supporting influential parents, being unwilling to make negative evaluation, chastising the entire staff instead of individual(s) responsible, . . . hiding in the office, and prefacing requests with 'the board wants' or 'the superintendent wants'" (p. 18).

A first step for the principal is gathering information about his performance so that he can recognize his shortcomings and their potential impact on the school. A self-evaluation such as the one provided in Resource D may assist the principal in this process. With increased information about his performance, the principal will be in a position to develop a plan of action for addressing his weaknesses.

The Job

In order that people may be happy in their work, these things are needed: They must be fit for it: They must not do too much of it: And they must have a sense of success in it.

John Ruskin
Pre-Raphaelitism (1851)

The work of the principal is often fragmented. For individuals who lack managerial skills, the principalship may be an incredible challenge.

The examples of mistakes in this chapter reflect the endless work experienced by principals. Coupled with the endless work are the mistakes that emerge when time constraints hinder a principal's performance. The endless work and time constraints are definitely related to one another. The discussion and suggestions that follow the examples focus on organizational skills that can be enlisted to manage the workload and respond to time constraints.

Mistake 8
Endless Work

The work of the principalship is often described as seemingly endless. Linked to the work are the time constraints that principals report. The mistakes that emerge when principals do not confront the seamless Möbius strip of these two issues are noted in the following examples.

Scenario 24: Overwhelmed

> *Principals described the mistake they made by being overwhelmed by their work. They described being at work from 6:30 in the morning until late at night—and feeling like they always needed to be at work. Not doing enough, not being able to catch up with the work, and not being able to walk away from the work were examples of their dilemmas. The lament of not being able "to get it all done" was frequent. They spoke of being responsible for solving every issue.*

Rχ: For principals, one school year may be indistinguishable from any other school year. The August-September to May-June cycle simply repeats itself annually. Principals who allow themselves to be swept into this cycle see no future in their work. Principals need benchmarks so that they can measure progress toward goals. School should not be an endless cycle of sameness. If principals are hopeless, then teachers and students will be hopeless too.

The principals in this scenario reflect hopelessness. For survival, the principal needs to break the work up into a series of tasks. Each day the principal needs to identify which tasks will be accomplished. Task accomplishment should signal the completion of a day's work.

Keeping a log of what is accomplished each day for at least a week would help this individual. Using this information, a principal should then be able to identify what can realistically be accomplished in a day.

The only person who can control the principal's work is the principal. The principal must put boundaries around the day by specifying the work to be accomplished in that day. Without a clear vision for what must be accomplished, the principal never will find a "stopping place." The principal should not allow the length of the work day to expand without experiencing the satisfaction of task completion. The principal needs to be reminded that "Spirit and faith are the core of human life. Without them, you lose your way. You live without zest. You go through the motions, but there's no passion" (Bolman & Deal, 1995, p. 20). Only the principal can correct this situation.

There is so much work to be done in a school that the tasks can be overwhelming. A principal who does not have clear goals can waste considerable effort doing whatever task is near at hand.

The work of the school must be viewed in terms of what is most important—what work will achieve the goals of the school. There is work that only the principal can do and there is work that can be delegated. The principal must delegate work to the other responsible individuals in the school. By reviewing and redistributing administrative responsibilities, the principal is providing other individuals with opportunities to develop their leadership skills. The principal should work to be in the background, not on center stage.

If there are assistant principals or other administrative assistants available, the principal should organize the office so that these other administrators can handle the line of people at the principal's door. Delegation could reduce the demands on the principal.

A lack of confidence may make a principal's work harder than it already is. A principal needs to have a vision for the school. The vision should form the basis for the school's goals.

The goals provide direction for what should be accomplished on a daily basis. Setting reasonable expectations for each day is the principal's responsibility. With practice, the principal will become more adept at planning a day's work. At the end of each day, the principal should be able to document the day's accomplishments. These accomplishments signal the completion of a day's work. As evidence of accomplishments increase, the principal's confidence should increase. This will allow the principal to experience closure to school work and permit the principal to leave the school with a clear conscience.

Bergman's (1992) "Lessons for Principals" should help the principal "let go."

1. Learn to listen

2. Establish patterns for communication

3. Understand individual styles

4. Promote open communication

5. Work to build trust

6. Think with new perspectives

7. Promote autonomy, "Let Go"

8. Take time for self-reflection.

Being superhuman is not part of the principal's job. Realizing that the principal can only do so much, and that no one is perfect, is a reasonable way to approach the principalship. Setting the stage at the beginning of the school year by identifying expectations and limitations should be part of the principal's agenda.

Scenario 25: Learning on the Job

Principals reported the mistakes they made while learning what was important in the job. Mastering the position took longer than they anticipated and they said they may have made the job even more difficult than it was. They experienced new challenges such as learning to work with others, like secretaries.

Rχ: Although university preparation programs exist, they cannot prepare principals for the uniqueness of each school. In spite of the best efforts of the preparation programs, much of the principalship is learned on the job.

Before assuming a new principalship, an individual needs to gather information about the school, the community, the teachers, and the staff. It is important to spend time with individuals who know about the school. Time spent individually with teachers will provide tremendous insight into the culture and character of the school. Each person may have a personal agenda for the principal or for the items to be changed. Principals listen, but should not act on anything until full information is available. Often the secretary can provide critical information that makes the job doable.

Individuals who become principals may not have had experience working with a secretary. These individuals may not understand the type and amount of work a secretary can accomplish.

Individuals who have worked in situations where secretaries were unskilled, unwilling, or underutilized may not know how to work with a secretary. In situations such as these, principals learn how to simultaneously manage their work and the secretary's work. In time, these individuals cease looking to the secretary for assistance, because their earlier experiences have been unsatisfactory.

Secretaries bring specialized skills to their work. Identifying secretarial strengths and maximizing those strengths to accomplish the school's work is the principal's challenge. Secretaries, like other staff members, need to be challenged, motivated, and recognized.

The secretary is often the first point of contact when people come to the school or call. Therefore the secretary needs to have strong public relations skills. The secretary can be the greatest asset a principal and a school have.

Principals may encounter the phenomena of the "all-powerful" secretary. They may find their secretaries "willing to help all the time" and "probably the reason I've been able to stay here this long." It is essential for principals to know about the secretary or secretaries they will inherit. The secretary can be the key to the long tenure or rapid departure for the principal (Grady, 2000).

The expectation for a newly hired principal is that that individual will "hit the ground running." In order to accomplish this, the principal must understand the vision for the school. Using the school's vision, the principal can then identify the goals that will guide the principal's work. The vision and goals allow the principal to identify the important and the unimportant aspects of the job. The principal must remember that a school is a complex organization and the principal should allow adequate time to understand the school and the job.

Mistake 9
Mismanaging Time

Time constraints are the companion issue to endless work. Both issues challenge principals. The lament about "lack of time" is heard from adults from many fields. When individuals do not address time issues, then their stress increases and their health may be compromised. Time management requires management of "self."

Scenario 26: Open Door

Principals described the mistake of allowing time eaters to consume their days. An open office door was viewed as both a benefit and a liability depending on who came through the door. Paperwork was a challenge that could not be mastered when there was a steady stream of office visitors.

Principals described how they came to work early in the morning so they could get more paperwork finished. They reported coming in on the weekends to accomplish more work. Often they said that the teachers came to school during these times seeking to visit with the principal.

The principals said they did not know how to encourage communication while having time to complete other administrative tasks. Their time was limited and their inability to manage all the tasks was troubling to them.

Rχ: A principal needs to maintain an open door to those who need attention. The secretary is a key resource in controlling access to the principal's office. The secretary can visit with individuals to determine their needs. Not all needs require the principal's attention. Staff need to be made aware of the demands on a principal's time.

"The early bird catches the worm" may not be the best maxim for the principal. Coming to work early is a practice designed to provide quiet time to accomplish the clerical tasks of the principalship. However, teachers look for opportunities to visit with the principal about their concerns. If they realize that the principal comes to school early, they will begin lining up at the principal's door early. When the principal fails to arrive, they are disappointed and possibly frustrated.

When the string of early visitors gets too long, the principal may need to abandon the early morning routine and search for other quiet time. The challenge of finding uninterrupted quiet time while meeting teachers' needs is constant.

Principals should be open and honest with faculty and staff about the need for quiet time to complete required paperwork. Teachers may have no understanding of the demands of the principal's job. Principals need to describe their work so that their efforts for the school and students are recognized and respected.

A principal needs time with family or just time at home without work. Teachers should learn to respect the principal's need to have time behind closed doors. During times when the principal's door is closed, the secretary needs to tell the teachers when the principal will be available.

Principal success is often based on a good flow of information, and information flows through the principal's door. Building strong relationships is essential to developing a positive school culture and accomplishing school goals. The principal builds relationships by working with staff and parents. What may appear as "socializing" may in fact be the most important work that a principal does.

Teachers must have access to the principal. However, time management is essential to the success of a principal. The open door policy must be handled carefully to assure that all of the principal's objectives are met.

Good public relations are exceptionally valuable. Principals must greet people and informally visit with people, yet be skillful in resuming tasks. It is the fine art of using all time effectively and efficiently. Consider the following list of time wasters:

- Steady stream of unscheduled visitors
- Random telephone calls
- Overused e-mail
- Disorganization
- Failure to delegate
- Lack of goals
- Unrealistic timelines or expectations
- Avoiding decision making
- Incomplete information

Leaders need a road map. "If you don't know where you're going, it's hard to know when you get there!" Principals, like everyone else, get to plan a 24-hour day. What a principal accomplishes in a day is based on planning and goals as well as persistence in working toward those goals. What is accomplished represents the choices made during a day. In many cases, too much time is spent on the details and too little time is spent on the main functions of the school. A principal's choices reflect conscious decisions as well as intentional neglect. Principals tend to do what they want to do. A principal's inaction is as much a choice as a principal's action.

Scenario 27: Endless "To Do" Lists

The principal described her frustration at what she was able to accomplish in a day. She described having "to do" lists that were endless. She said that she was expected to respond to everyone's demands. She noted how dissatisfied she was with her performance because she was not accomplishing what she thought she should.

Rχ: The demands of the principalship are seemingly without end. Even when these demands are prioritized, there is more to be done than can be accomplished by one person. The principal must adopt a strategy for managing the work. The key to the strategy is deciding how time will be apportioned.

As a starting point, effective leaders who reach their potential spend more time focusing on what they do well than on what they do wrong. According to Maxwell (1999), to be successful, one must focus on strengths and develop them. Time, energy, and resources should be "poured into" the development of strengths.

Maxwell (1999) also recommends "shifting to strengths." To do this, identify three or four things that you do well. Then, determine what percentage of your time is spent doing these things. Then, determine what percentage of the resources are dedicated to these strengths. Next, devise a plan to make changes so that 70% of your time can be invested in these strengths.

As an extension of this plan to use time more effectively, Maxwell (1999) recommended "staffing your weaknesses." To do this, identify three or four activities that you do not do well. Then, determine how you can delegate these tasks to someone else. Develop a plan so that the delegation occurs. These strategies should help the principal in this scenario achieve greater satisfaction with her work.

Eleanor Roosevelt (1960) wrote about the uses of time. Her approach should be useful to this principal as well.

> We have all the time there is. The problem is: How shall we make the best use of it? There are three ways in which I have been able to solve that problem: first, by achieving an inner calm so that I can work undisturbed by what goes on around me; second, by concentrating on the thing in hand; third, by arranging a routine pattern for my days that allots certain activities to certain hours, planning in advance for everything that must be done, but at the same time remaining flexible enough to allow for the unexpected. There is a fourth point which, perhaps, plays a considerable part in the use of my time. I try to maintain a general pattern of good health so that I have the best use of my energy whenever I need it. (pp. 45–46)

Tasks

Do not pray for easy lives. Pray to be stronger men (and women)! Do not pray for tasks equal to your powers. Pray for powers equal to your tasks.

Phillips Brooks
Sermons, Going Up to Jerusalem

The principal is responsible for a broad array of tasks. In this chapter, principals' mistakes in the areas of preparation, goal setting, decision making, and supervision are presented. A discussion and suggestions for improving performance in these areas are presented as well.

Mistake 10
Ignoring the Preparation

Before moving to a new principalship, it is best to invest time in examining the conditions at the school and in the community. The value of this early reconnaissance is a smoother transition and possibly greater stability in the position.

Scenario 28: Doing Your Homework

> *One principal described entering a really toxic environment in his first principalship. He said there was considerable animosity and divisiveness between the principal and the staff. He described being sabotaged at every step.*

Rχ: During the interview, the principal should gather information about the school and the staff. Questions about the school, the staff, the climate, and the effectiveness of the school's program should be asked.

The candidate should identify the causes of principal turnover during the past 10 years. All of this information should be acquired before one agrees to assume a principalship.

> Find out as much as possible about your predecessors and where the "land mines" are. Whether you are following someone who was successful or are replacing someone who was not a "good fit" with the school, you should find out as much as possible about your school's feelings toward your predecessor. This will give you much guidance about what you should do and, equally important, what you should not do. (Skelly, 1996, p. 93)

If an individual decides to accept a principalship in a difficult situation, then the information gathered before and during the interview can be used to develop a plan and strategies to use on the job. A toxic environment cannot be remedied in a short time. The new principal needs to develop a long-term plan to transform the negative environment.

The principal needs to get to know all the teachers. Face-to-face conversations and reviewing existing documents will assist in the process. All of the staff should be asked what is and what is not working in the school.

The school environment can be transformed by various measures. Changes in schedules or in classrooms can alter the dynamics of the interactions in a school. Changes in teaching assignments can precipitate changes in behaviors. Changes in the cycle of meetings and how the meetings are organized can alter the conversations in a school.

Principals who clearly articulate the goals of the school help teachers decide if they are in the right setting or not. Persistently emphasizing the school goals and linking all activities and all conversations to those goals reduces the opportunities for conversations that are not supportive of the school or principal. Teacher appraisal must be linked to goal accomplishment. Teachers who are not accomplishing the school goals need to be made aware of their deficiencies and helped to achieve the school goals. Teachers who do not want to work toward school goals may choose to work in other settings. Many principals will leave a principalship rather than work with a faculty that is not goal oriented.

Scenario 29: Insiders vs. Outsiders

One individual reported moving into a principalship after being a teacher and a team leader in the same building for a long time. He knew the staff really well. His mistake was ignoring the good staff members while he was stomping out fires.

Rx: Moving into the principalship in a building where an individual has worked as a teacher or team leader for a number of years has its own challenges. The principal is well known and has developed friendships with many staff members. As the principal, it may be necessary to establish some professional distance from old friends. It may be difficult to make decisions because of the influence of friendships. The "insider" principal may not be taken as seriously as an "outsider" principal would be. The "insider" principal must always contend with the staff who "knew you when."

Carlson (1962) identified two types of administrators—placebound and careerbound. Placebound administrators are insiders who work within a school system until the highest position is achieved. Careerbound administrators are outsiders who seek positions wherever they are to be found.

> Carlson's analysis of the social system confronting insiders is also relevant for the new principals. Insiders face social systems that are established, well-defined, structured, and relatively unaltered, while outsiders face social systems that have been temporarily suspended because of their arrival. Outsiders, therefore, have an advantage with respect to organizational development and adaptation because they initially have the opportunity to maneuver and to reshape the structure and norms of social systems. (Hoy & Miskel, 2000, p. 156)

In this case, the principal knows the faculty strengths and leaves those who are doing a good job "on their own." The issue is that each member of the professional staff deserves and seeks the principal's attention. Passive neglect is harmful to the climate of the school.

"Stomping out fires" is not the desirable image of the work of the principal. The principal should be working toward achieving the vision for the school. Minor management issues should not consume the principal's work day because they distract the principal from the significant work of the school.

Mistake 11
Displacing Goals

Goals provide the roadmap for success. Visionary leaders are noted for the prominence of their goals in the schools. Organizational effectiveness is defined in terms of goal attainment. Goals provide the priority list for the work that should be "done first."

Scenario 30: High Expectations

> *A fatal mistake a principal can make is not having high expectations for kids. The abilities of the kids can be wasted. The principal and the teachers must strive for the best for kids.*

Rχ: What is achieved by students and teachers is a direct result of expectations. Expectations must be high and it is the principal's responsibility to establish those expectations.

Expectations become the basis for goals in the school. The goals must reflect the culture of the community, be prominently displayed, and repeated frequently. All should know what is valued in the school. The expectations must be reinforced at every opportunity. Stating them on banners, newsletters, restating them at meetings, and holding special events focused on them are means of promoting the attainment of goals in the school. Celebrations and special recognitions should accompany the achievement of goals. Students, teachers, and families need to share in the work of achieving the goals.

When entering a school, the culture is tangible. Wheatley (1993) offered the following description. "To a person, we agreed that we could 'feel' good customer service just by walking into the store. . . . We could feel it, we just couldn't describe why we felt it" (p. 53). High expectations are prominent in a school's atmosphere.

Individuals preparing to be principals should concentrate on the importance of developing vision.

> If vision is a field, think about what we could do differently to create one. We would do our best to get it permeating through the entire organization so that we could take advantage of its formative properties. All employees, in any part of the company, who bumped up against that field could be influenced by it. Their behavior could be shaped as a result of "field meetings," where their energy would link with the field's form to create behavior congruent with the organization's goals. (Wheatley, 1993, p. 54)

A principal's vision must include high expectations for students. Keeping the focus on the vision is a constant task for the principal.

Scenario 31: The Leaderless Group

Teachers described their principal as always spending a lot of time having meetings with the teachers. They are constantly in the process of implementing new programs or procedures. During meetings the principal takes notes and tells the teachers she will report back to them. The teachers complained that they never see anything from those meetings or those notes. They said there's never any follow-up or continuity—one initiative after another is dropped.

Rx: A generous interpretation would be that the principal may be overwhelmed by her job. However, the truth may be that she lacks either the time or the ability to implement these initiatives.

New initiatives can be very exciting to those trying to meet student needs. Innovations are suggested by teachers, principals, state departments of education, and legislative mandates. It is easy to see how schools can be overwhelmed by innovations. Although innovations are well intended, they demand time and attention. It takes years to fully implement an innovation.

The principal should identify the number of innovations that are being implemented in the school. This principal should beware of fitting this analogy: "He needed movement as the shark does; it was his way of breathing" (Wills, 1994, p. 92). A conversation with teachers would indicate the status of these innovations. The time needed to fully implement each innovation should be understood and reflected in the change cycle.

Innovations that are dictated by the district office, state, or legislature are not choices. However, innovations that originate at the school level should be examined to determine whether they should be pursued or not. "Fads in schools seem to arrive like ocean waves striking a beach. They crash on shore with great ferocity and strength, but then they somehow sink back into the depths from whence they came" (Hanson, 2003, p. 319). Discussions with the faculty should focus on what is best for kids and how faculty time should be used to meet student needs.

The principal may need to learn to "let go." Occasionally individuals fear the loss of power or authority. They fail to delegate responsibilities to other qualified members of the staff. If initiatives or directives are coming too frequently, the principal needs to communicate this to the central office.

The principal's lack of follow-through and organizational know-how is having a negative effect on the faculty. The faculty's willingness to engage in the "endless" meeting and discussion cycle will wane. Faculty frustration and disgruntlement can destroy the learning environment. Fullan (1988) noted that "effective leaders have 'a bias for action.' They have an overall sense of direction, and start into action as soon as possible establishing small scale examples, adapting, refining, improving quality, expanding, and reshaping as the process unfolds" (p. 26–27).

Without a vision and goals, the principal and staff lack direction. The staff must have a basis for making decisions and know what it is that they are working toward.

This principal should review Wills' (1994) description of leadership. "Most literature on leadership is Unitarian. But life is Trinitarian. One-legged and two-legged chairs do not, of themselves, stand. A third leg is needed. Leaders, followers, and goals make up the three equally necessary supports for leadership" (p. 17).

Scenario 32: Instructional Leadership

Principals noted that their biggest mistake was not getting into the classrooms. They said that it was really hard to get into the classrooms or out into the building. They described being inundated with paperwork and spending too little time with teachers in classrooms.

Rχ: Supervision is the principal's responsibility. Supervision is helping teachers improve instruction for students (Glickman, 2003). Blumberg (1986) noted, "As is supervision so will be the schools" (p. 7). Time spent on this task will be well spent.

Since principals have a finite amount of time in a workday, successful principals establish goals and priorities for tasks. The annual deadline for completing classroom appraisals is known, and classroom visits should be planned accordingly. Principals who have a clear commitment to teacher observation make this task a priority. It is first on the list.

To accomplish a goal, the goal must be acknowledged every day. If the primary goal is to be in the classrooms, then it has to be first on the principal's list. Principals must determine exactly how much time they want to spend in each classroom. A schedule must be established that meets the goals for classroom observations. In addition, time must be set aside for discussions of these observations with the teachers.

The principals' frustration is understandable. The principalship and its many demands can be overwhelming. Everyone who visits the principal's office or calls adds to the demands that compete for the principal's attention. Only the principal can change the situation described here. The first step is for the principal to identify daily goals that must be accomplished, and then exercise the commitment to achieve the goals. Delegation of tasks would reduce the paperwork. A review of all paperwork may result in new insights about how to reorder or eliminate some aspects of the work. Better processes or better organization may be helpful in managing these tasks.

Former U.S. President Jimmy Carter (1996) reported using the following process for analyzing his behavior.

> I try to ask myself three key questions: Are the goals I am pursuing appropriate? Am I doing the right thing, based on my personal moral code, my Christian faith, and the duties of my current position? And finally, have I done my best, based on the alternatives open to me? (p. 104–105)

According to Tirozzi (2001), the principals of tomorrow's schools will be recognized as leaders of curricular change, innovation and diversified instructional strategies, data-driven decision making, and the implementation of accountability models for students and staff.

Principals will:

- Set the tone for their buildings
- Facilitate the teaching and learning process
- Provide leadership and direction to their school's instructional programs and policies
- Spend significantly more time evaluating staff and mentoring new teachers
- Sustain professional development for themselves and their staff members
- Nurture personalized school environments for all students (Tirozzi, 2001, p. 438)

Mistake 12
Decision-Making Dilemmas

The principal is often expected to display the wisdom of Solomon when making decisions. Although some principals may have natural decision-making skills, other principals must develop these skills through practice and patience. Seeking information, listening to the involved individuals, acting in a timely manner, sharing responsibility, and avoiding emotional responses are all aspects of the principal's role in decision making.

Scenario 33: Quick Draw

Principals noted the mistakes they made when they were pressured to make decisions. They reported being trapped by expectations to provide rapid responses. By "reacting," they found themselves backed into corners.

Rχ: One important reminder is that not every person who confronts the principal with an issue needs an answer. Sometimes simply listening is sufficient. Skelly (1996) suggested the following. "It may be liberating to you personally and helpful professionally to begin your tenure by often saying things like 'I don't know,' and 'I want to do as much listening as possible,' and 'I need your help'" (pp. 92–93).

The principal's office is not an emergency room where patients need immediate care. Principals may feel pressured to reach hasty decisions. Being able to mentally back away from the individual presenting the issue will provide perspective and the opportunity to consider alternatives. Saying simply, "I'll get back to you" or "I'll investigate this" can protect a principal from the pressure to make a rapid decision. If at all possible, make it a rule to "sleep on it" before making an important decision.

The "firefighter" approach to decision making may not be the best approach. Some principals run from problem to problem giving quick responses to what are perceived as emergency situations. Fortunately, the school is not a house on fire.

The issues that deserve the principal's primary attention are those that are about the students. These issues concern teaching and learning as well as the well-being of students. Student issues should not be treated as fires that need to be extinguished. Student issues deserve the best professional knowledge and attention.

Principals need to listen to the students about their issues. Sometimes students have a better understanding of what transpires in the building, playground, lunchroom, and classroom than any of the adults do. Care and consideration are the terms that should pertain to students.

These principals are experiencing one of the conundrums of the principalship. People have little patience when they want an answer. Yet "quick" answers often are wrong answers or bad decisions.

Principals must clearly state a commitment to answering questions and making decisions. However, they must also clearly state that good decisions and accurate answers may take time. If principals are consistent and equitable in responding to individuals, then they will, in time, be trusted to reach decisions as quickly as possible. In order to earn this trust, the principals must be sure to follow up with promised decisions. Individuals who have been "forgotten" will not trust them.

Maxwell (1999) described competent individuals in the following summary:

When you think about people who are competent, you're really considering only three types of people:

1. Those who can see what needs to happen.

2. Those who can make it happen.

3. Those who can make things happen when it really counts. (p. 35)

Scenario 34: Avoidance

Some principals described their biggest mistakes as trying to avoid making decisions. Their approach was to hope that issues would just work themselves out if given enough time. They talked about trying to keep everything calm and smooth.

Rχ: Sometimes things will just "work themselves out." Sometimes individuals who approach the principal with concerns just want to be heard. Having an audience is all that is needed.

However, there is a time to listen and there is a time to take action. The principal's role is an action position. Principals must answer questions and address concerns. Passive neglect can be disastrous for a school. Having a reputation as a weak or do-nothing principal will cause many problems. When a principal allows a leadership vacuum to develop the vacuum will be filled—by teachers in the school. When this occurs, the legitimate authority of the principal is undermined. The principal becomes powerless.

The principals in this scenario need to take charge. Keeping a log of questions and concerns and documenting the answers or resolutions is a starting point. Keeping in constant communication with individuals who have concerns is critical. Decision-making skills improve with practice.

A calm and smooth environment is possibly a stagnant environment. Doing everything the same way it's always been done is a way to avoid change. Principals need to be able to tolerate an upheaval in the daily functioning of the school, and be able to endure the conflict that may accompany decisions or change. Change has the potential to create conflict and controversy—a turbulent environment. However, stagnation leads to withering. In a school, this would mean a lack of progress and growth. For students and teachers, this approach could lead to the extinction of motivation and creativity.

The needs of students are rapidly changing and require dynamic responses, and dynamic decisive leadership. "A leader can give up anything—except final responsibility" (Maxwell, 1999, p. 111).

Scenario 35: The Center of the Universe

Some principals have to be the "first one to know everything." Although they have department chairs and vice principals, all decisions come directly from the principals; all information has to be filtered through them. In some cases it appears that they are too emotionally and personally entangled in the work of the school.

Rχ: It is ironic that many principals work in school situations where they have way too many kids with way too many needs. These principals would relish the help that could be provided by one assistant principal. The principals in this scenario, who are compelled to control decisions, are wasting the talents of the other administrators.

School issues are many and complex. Dividing the work, the responsibility, and the authority would allow each of the administrators an equitable share in the work. The administrators would have the opportunity to focus on and develop an area of expertise. More could be accomplished for the children if all the expertise in the school was fully employed.

Vienne (1998) offered an alternative approach to the behavior of the principals in this scenario:

The next time you attend a meeting, sit back, relax, listen. Be the designated listener. Note how much concentration it takes just to follow every word of a verbal exchange.

You don't have to talk to be an active participant: As far as others are concerned, every one of your glances, head movements, smiles, or facial expressions is part of what is being said.

The more you listen to others, the more they will seek your approval. Vigilance is a powerful magnet. When focused, your attention acts as the baton of a conductor. Silently, you can orchestrate the flow of ideas, influence the outcome of the conversation—or add to the confusion. Whoever listens most usually controls the situation. (pp. 76–78)

The principals who must be "in control" need to consider their beliefs about the teachers and administrators in their schools. Their beliefs are affecting the way they are working with these professionals.

Douglas McGregor and Abraham Maslow implored leaders to look into the mirror and question their assumptions. Their questions were

1. Do you believe that people are trustworthy?

2. Do you believe that people seek responsibility and accountability?

3. Do you believe that people seek meaning in their work?

4. Do you believe that people naturally want to learn?

5. Do you believe that people don't resist change but they resist being changed?

6. Do you believe that people prefer work to being idle? (Maslow, 1998, p. 15)

The answers to these questions affect everything that a principal does. Many principals never take the time to analyze their assumptions about people. Perhaps principals who must be "the center of the universe" should consider these questions.

Scenario 36: Emotions

Some principals were too emotionally wound up in situations and decisions. They said they often lost perspective on situations and conflicts because they did not have enough distance from the issue.

Rx: Principals need to establish professional space between themselves and their work. Unfortunately, some individuals transform their work lives into their personal lives. This may not be a healthy approach to the principalship.

The best decisions are reached when one has some detachment from the individuals and the situations. The principal needs to see the big picture, to have a broad perspective, and to understand the impact of a decision on the whole school. Principals need to develop a personal life separate from their work at school, and be detached from direct personal entanglements in school issues.

Tooms (2003) suggests that principals follow their own "compass" by considering the following:

- Own what you are responsible for—let the rest go
- How you see yourself is not how you are seen
- Don't mistake calm waters for safe, shark-free waters
- You can build strong professional relationships without confiding your secrets and weaknesses
- Loyalty is not automatic—with anyone (Tooms, 2003, p. 533)

Mistake 13
Change Dilemmas

Change is a natural and constant part of organizational life. Change can enrich the organizational life and the instructional life of a school. Principals who perfect the art of implementing and managing change have the ability to create positive learning environments.

Scenario 37: Tradition

One woman, as a new principal, made many changes at the school. Many "old traditions" were eliminated. She did not recognize the impact of her actions. Through her inexperience, her actions caused considerable damage to the culture of the school.

R𝝌: Traditions bind groups together. They represent the people and the history of the school. They help to define a place and its uniqueness. Bolman and Deal (1995) described the significance of ritual and ceremony to a community:

When ritual and ceremony are authentic and attuned, they fire the imagination, evoke insight, and touch the heart. Ceremony weaves past, present, and future into life's ongoing tapestry. Ritual helps us to face and comprehend life's everyday shocks, triumphs, and mysteries. Both ritual and ceremony help us experience the unseen webs of significance that tie a community together. (p. 111)

Principals must be sensitive to and considerate of the customs and traditions that exist in their schools. By visiting with teachers, staff, and students, much can be learned about the rituals and traditions that are important in the school.

Fullan (2001) offers "six guidelines that provide leaders with concrete and novel ways of thinking about the process of change:

1. The goals is not to innovate the most

2. It is not enough to have the best ideas

3. Appreciate early difficulties of trying something new

4. Redefine resistance as a potential positive force

5. Reculturing is the name of the game" (p. 5)

Before any changes are made, a principal needs to have carefully analyzed the pros and cons of the proposed change. Teachers and others need to be involved in the change process from the beginning. Only in this way can a principal build support for a change and assure that the change will be properly implemented. Some changes take a very long time.

When people are given information, opportunity to learn, and trust to make changes, unusual results become possible. Much of the improvement comes from the feeling of self confidence people gain when they see how their efforts contribute to making a difference. (Wilkins, 1989, p. 187)

Principals can use properly implemented changes to enhance the culture and traditions of a school. Proper planning is essential to success in a change process.

Scenario 38: Easy (and Careful) Does It

The principal's mistakes were the drastic changes she made the first year she was here. She changed teaching assignments, schedules, and procedures. Many of these changes were made without consulting anyone.

R℞: Before any change is initiated, a principal should take time to get to know the staff and the school. Change takes time, patience, and persistence. Listening to the staff and building support are prerequisites to the initiation of change. Rooney (2000) identified the following principal's "facts of life":

The ghosts of the past still rule the school. Although invisible, the image of the last principal haunts the current leader. Even though school faculty and staff noted the principal's frailties while she ran the school, they endow her with saintly virtues once she leaves. The new leader must acknowledge and respect the ghosts of her predecessors. (p. 77)

When a staff is not involved in planning for change, then resistance to the change can be predicted. "Change comes slowly through strong relationships built with staff, parents, and students" (Rooney, 2000, p. 78). Teachers are entitled to participate in the change process, since they too are professionals. If change concerns curriculum and instruction, then the teachers must be part of the entire process.

Principals who fail to work collaboratively with teachers will stimulate conflict. Conflict with teachers can be very disruptive to the entire school program. Strong relationships provide the foundation for change.

Change should be a "life-giving" force in an organization. Wheatley (1993) described this force in the following passage:

> Once it was noted that systems were capable of exchanging energy, taking in free energy to replace the entropy that had been produced, scientists realized that deterioration was not inevitable. Disturbances could create disequilibrium, but disequilibrium could lead to growth. (p. 87)

For those who question change, there is the reminder that "Nothing endures but change" (Heraclitus c. 513 B.C.).

Mistake 14
Professional Development Vacuum

Principals make mistakes when they do not recognize the professional development needs of the faculty and staff. Without the revitalization offered by professional development activities, skills erode and enthusiasm wanes. Principals must secure the time and resources to make these opportunities possible.

Scenario 39: Assuming

Among the mistakes principals reported was assuming that teachers had the preparation they needed to be good teachers. Some potentially fine teachers left the profession because they were not given help in transitioning into their professional roles.

Other principals assumed that experienced teachers knew how to work with the students. They did not recognize that many teachers had had their university training years ago. Nothing had been offered to them as professional development to deal with current student issues. They had not had any special education training and they had not kept pace with the demographic changes in the schools.

Rχ: Teacher preparation programs take beginning teachers to the schoolhouse door. It is the principal's challenge to carry the teacher across the threshold and transform the beginner into a master teacher. The preparation program lays the rudimentary foundation for a teaching career. The principal's task is to help develop the teacher's professional skills.

In schools that have many students and many challenges, new teachers are often forgotten. This wastes the new teacher's abilities and often denies students a positive educational experience. New teachers must be supported and nurtured.

When teachers leave the teaching profession, a tremendous investment is lost. Recruitment and hiring processes are expensive. As new teachers begin their work in the schools, resources are invested in their "learning on the job." If teachers depart early in their careers, these investments are lost. Students' learning is disrupted by teacher turnover.

The number of identified special needs students in schools has increased. It is not unusual to discover that many teachers have never had any formal preparation to work with special needs students.

The students coming to the schools are different in many ways. Students may have physical challenges or behavioral issues. They may come from different family situations, different cultures, different socioeconomic backgrounds, or different countries or states. Teachers and principals must be prepared to meet the needs of this changing population.

Consider Figure 5.1, which represents the changes that have occurred in the makeup of families. How familiar are teachers with this portrait of the changing demographics of U.S. society? In addition to the shifts in the composition of families from 1950 to 1996, the following demographics describe the status of single-parent families: "Eighty-seven percent of single-parent families are headed by women and many of these families face poverty or new poverty" (Richards & Schmiege, 1993, p. 278).

It is the principal's responsibility to provide the faculty with the demographic information they need to understand

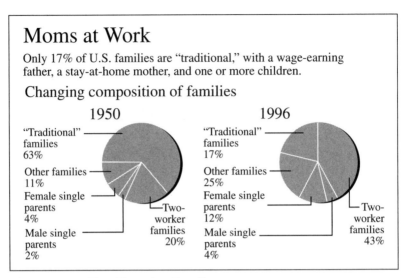

Moms at Work

Only 17% of U.S. families are "traditional," with a wage-earning father, a stay-at-home mother, and one or more children.

Changing composition of families

Figure 5.1   The Changing Family

SOURCE: Bureau of Labor Statistics, *Omaha World-Herald,* March 15, 1998,
        p. 1G

the students and their needs. Tirozzi (2001) reported the following demographics:

Hispanics and Asians will constitute 61% of the nation's population growth by 2025 . . . Forty-three million Americans move every year . . . The states with the highest percentages of students graduating from high school and being admitted to college are states with stable populations, while the most transient states have the lowest percentages of students graduating from high school and being admitted to college . . . The greatest demand for school construction will be in communities that have not even been named yet . . . as the nation's fastest-growing block of voters, the elderly will have greatly expanded power in the school finance arena. (p. 435)

Principals are responsible for maintaining a skilled faculty. Professional development opportunities provide teachers with new skills for their jobs. Assessing faculty needs should be the principal's first step in planning for professional development activities.

"The squeaky wheel gets the oil" may be a definite dilemma for a principal. The principal's challenge is to support or "oil" all of the faculty and staff. Crises or incompetent faculty members have a way of stealing the attention from the rest of the faculty. Keeping the focus on the entire professional staff must be the principal's commitment.

Whitaker (1997) provided the following summary of the importance of the teachers and the principal's role as an instructional leader:

> The teachers in the schools are its greatest resource, and they must be acknowledged for exemplary teaching and encouraged to share with others. The principal must know the strengths and weaknesses of the teachers and show genuine concern for their health, welfare, and professional growth. This caring approach creates a faculty willing to take risks and approach change positively. (p. 155)

Scenario 40: Stagnation

> *Teachers identified the constraints at their school. They said they did not have any support for professional development activities and were not permitted to attend meetings outside of school. No money was available for training opportunities. There was no encouragement or support for those who were working on graduate degrees.*

Rχ: These teachers' comments echo Blanchard and Johnson's (1983) statement that "Most companies spend more time and money on maintaining their buildings and equipment than they do on maintaining and developing people" (p. 45). Fostering and encouraging professional growth for faculty is the principal's responsibility. Although districts exist where there are no financial resources available to support teacher attendance at workshops, motivated principals can design action research projects and arrange learning partnerships among the faculty to provide minimal cost growth opportunities. Not all guest speakers charge fees. Faced with these challenges, successful principals demonstrate creativity and finesse.

There are school districts that restrict or limit teacher absences so that the teachers are always with the students. In these situations, principals must find ways to stimulate faculty development within the strictures imposed by school district policies.

Learning communities provide ways for everyone, regardless of their role, to form teams. These teams of adults can work collaboratively in structures that enable them to share responsibility for student learning. Strategies like study groups, peer coaching, and collective assessment of student work ensure that learning is a focused and ongoing process. In this way, the teacher's day-to-day work becomes a form of high quality professional development. Establishing a learning community is a worthwhile effort that can result in a more coherent, focused atmosphere—an atmosphere that encourages committed educators to continue to grow through trust, respect, and collegiality (Haar, 2001a).

Principals must ensure that professional growth needs are met and that schools are infused with the best in educational practice. Professional networks should be developed and maintained and professional associations should be encouraged. The messages from the principals must be continuously repeated so that the faculty understands the importance of pursuing professional development opportunities.

Mistake 15
Failing to Supervise

Supervision is a key administrative task. Principals who do not have supervisory skills or who fail to embrace their supervisory roles make mistakes that are readily recognized by the teachers.

Scenario 41: Going Through the Motions

Some teachers said that their principal just seems to go through the motions when it comes time to evaluate teachers. New teachers may be evaluated once or twice a year, but teachers who have been in the system for years are not being evaluated.

Other teachers from different schools described individual teachers who needed the principal's attention. They spoke of a teacher who constantly screamed at students and intimidated them. They described situations where teachers left their classrooms unsupervised.

Rχ: An essential principal responsibility is teacher evaluation. When a principal appears to be avoiding this responsibility, or if the principal lacks competence in teacher evaluation, then assistance from someone knowledgeable about evaluation techniques should be sought.

Teacher evaluation is a positive, life-giving force in a school when it is used to identify teacher strengths and areas of weakness. Teacher evaluation should be based on goals for professional improvement. Principals assist teachers in attempting to achieve those goals. Teacher evaluation should not be an adversarial relationship between the teacher and principal.

Occasionally a principal's lack of involvement in evaluation may be the result of time management and planning difficulties. The principal needs to examine priorities and assure that teacher evaluation assumes prominence in the work day.

Principals must be constantly vigilant. The principal's responsibility is to be aware of teacher behaviors and to confront behaviors that are harmful to the students.

More experienced teachers may need special attention. Since their university preparation was completed, the school-aged population has changed. New teaching techniques for the new generation of students may be needed. Providing staff development opportunities would be helpful.

The principal needs to be aware of all aspects of the school and take action to ensure the safety of the students. Being visible in the school is a first step. Walking through the school halls provides the principal with information about where the students and the teachers are. Monitoring the halls and the teachers' presence in the classrooms is an important part of creating safe schools. Unsupervised students represent opportunities for accidents and problems.

On occasion, teachers will use school as their adult, social contact. Meeting adult affiliation needs should not take precedence over meeting student needs. Teachers may need to be reminded of the purpose of school. Those who are not attentive to student needs must be made aware of their shortcomings.

Scenario 42: Escape Route

The teachers said the principal did not monitor the kids leaving school during the day. The kids escaped by running through a field adjacent to the school. Every day they could see the kids leaving. Even though they reported this, nothing was done about it.

Rχ: Providing adequate supervision is a critical task. Procedures must be in place to ensure the safety of all students. A principal's failure to plan for student safety can have deadly consequences. When teachers' reports of student safety concerns are unheeded, this poses a serious situation. Consequences for students can be unfortunate. Consequences for principals' careers can be fatal.

Staff support in enforcing school policies must be enlisted. In many cases, staff members may be closer to the problem than the principal is. Staff interventions could eliminate many potentially problematic situations. By enlisting staff support, the principal does not become the "middle person" in the resolution of the problem.

Many schools employ individuals as campus supervisors, to monitor the school grounds both inside and outside. These individuals patrol the halls, the parking lots, and are alert for students leaving the school grounds without permission. By employing supervisors to oversee this task, the burdens of student supervision are reduced for the administrators and teachers.

This scenario illustrates a potentially dangerous situation for students. When the teachers inform the principal of the situation and the principal fails to address the problem, then the principal is essentially refusing to do the work of a principal. Providing a safe school environment and supervising students are essential principal responsibilities. Working with teachers and staff to achieve these objectives is the principal's job. A plan for student supervision must be established. The principal must monitor the implementation and enforcement of the plan.

Scenario 43: Who's Incompetent?

The teachers described the principal ignoring incompetent teachers. The home economics teacher, who had taught in the school for 30 years, was an alcoholic. The principal did nothing about this.

The Spanish teacher either slept through class or was in a state of confusion. The students constantly mocked him.

Rχ: The principal makes a mistake by not knowing what is happening in classrooms and not knowing the condition of the teaching staff. This scenario suggests that the principal has failed to monitor performance in the classrooms, or has chosen to ignore poor performance.

When teachers have taught for a long time, principals may be reluctant to terminate their careers due to their diminished performance. Passive neglect has an insidious effect on a school. Principals must keep in mind that the purpose of schooling is student learning, not job security for teachers. The principal has the responsibility for revitalizing teachers who have lost their teaching zest. Blumberg (1986) reported a case of such a transformation:

Some of our old teachers . . . who imagined themselves masters of their trade, have recently found out their mistake . . . one remarked to me not long since, "I have kept school a great many winters, but now I am going to see if I cannot *teach* school." (p. 9–10)

For a principal, a case such as the one reported by Blumberg should be a reminder of why the principalship is a job worth having.

One incompetent teacher can rob the students of an entire year of schooling. Students cannot afford to lose a year to passive neglect.

Evaluation provides a framework for helping teachers develop their classroom management skills and improve their teaching skills. Principals may have difficulty communicating with teachers. They may fail to clearly articulate their expectations for teachers' performance. In their efforts to be kind, they may not make explicit the shortcomings in the teachers' performance.

The teachers have problems and need assistance. The other teachers in the school are aware of the principal's failure to address the problems. A principal who does not respond to these problems and needs signals "unfitness" for the principal's role.

By addressing the teachers' problems, the principal sends a message to all the teachers that inappropriate behavior will not be tolerated. Conscientious, professional teachers want issues such as these to be "handled." The person for the job is the principal.

The principal needs to document the teachers' behaviors and discuss that information with them. Drug treatment or medical treatment may be part of the improvement plan. The teachers should be provided with options to resolve the problems. The principal must then monitor the situations until they are satisfactorily resolved.

Personal Issues

My candle burns at both ends;
It will not last the night;
But, ah, my foes, and, oh, my friends—
It gives a lovely light.

Edna St. Vincent Millay
Figs from Thistles

Personal issues associated with the principalship are the focus of this section. The mistakes are related to health, stress, and family issues. Although personal issues are "private," little attention has been given to their impact on the principal's role. The personal life and the professional life being well ordered and complementary should be the principal's goal. A discussion and suggestions are provided for principals who seek to address the personal issues that may accompany the principal's work.

Mistake 16
Forgetting the Family

In the hustle and bustle of the principal's day, the principal's family may retreat into the background. Successful principals learn to balance their personal family life with their professional life.

Scenario 44: Family Time

Neglecting their families was a mistake principals reported. They described spending more time with everyone else's kids rather than with their own. Giving their best efforts and attention at school rather than at home was a shortcoming recounted by principals. Bringing work headaches home was noted as a way to create a rotten home environment.

Rx: The best support a principal has is the family. How to do the job well while keeping the family first is a constant challenge.

Many principals describe bringing their kids to school, or bringing their spouses and children to extracurricular activities with them. Planning and scheduling are essential if the principal is to meet both job and family expectations. Putting "first things first" is the principal's personal responsibility. Each person gets to choose priorities and make decisions based on those priorities. Family should always be the principal's first priority.

Having a personal life as a principal takes persistence. The principalship can gobble up every moment of a day. While the principal is tied to the job, the principal's children are growing up without a parent.

Spouses learn to live and manage without their principal mates. Most principals do not consider the cost to their personal lives when they take the job. They have not examined the impact of the principal's role on their spouses and children. Once principals recognize the potentially devastating personal cost of the principalship, they should take charge of their time and their priorities.

Leaving work at work and drawing boundaries between one's personal and professional lives requires real determination. When students are needy and schools have large enrollments, the likelihood of job overload is magnified. Only determination and commitment to being the best at home as well as at work will allow the principal to remedy this troubling condition. Scheduling work to accommodate both personal and professional goals is the clearest way to address this problem.

One way to improve organization is to make a list of what should be accomplished during the day. Throughout the day, refer to the list and check off items that are completed. Use Blanchard and Johnson's (1983) approach as a guide:

Take a Minute

Look at Your Goals

Look at Your Performance

See if Your Behavior Matches Your Goals (p. 74)

At the end of the day, review the list to identify the day's accomplishments. Items that were not accomplished become first on the next day's list. With practice, it will be possible to identify high priority items, as well as easier items that have a quick pay-off. There may also be items that take longer than a day to accomplish. At the end of a week, by reviewing these lists one can identify patterns of work and develop realistic expectations for what can be accomplished in a day.

A principal needs clear evidence of what is accomplished each day. With this information, it may be easier to leave school at the end of the day. Individuals who are uncertain about their accomplishments may find it more difficult to leave school.

Just as the day at work should be planned, the principal should plan the time outside of school. Family time and personal time deserve as much or more attention than school time.

> Those years, weeks, hours, are the sands in the glass running swiftly away. To let them drift through our fingers is a tragic waste. To use them to the hilt, making them count for something, is the beginning of wisdom. (Roosevelt, 1960, p. 60)

Scenario 45: Who Am I?

> *The principal said he was overwhelmed by his struggles with his work and personal life. He described being torn in too many directions. He said he was almost paralyzed by the demands and expectations in his life. He reported being constantly depressed because he was not accomplishing what he wanted to during the day.*

Rx: For this principal, just as for many talented adults, there are too many demands and opportunities in their lives. The pace of life is often frantic.

Few stop to consider the many roles they assume in their personal and professional lives. Figure 6.1 depicts possible roles a principal may assume. These roles intersect, overlap, and often lead to the situation referred to as overload.

As extensions of these roles, principals may find themselves serving as:

- Confidants
- Cheerleaders
- Decision makers
- Lovers

- Listeners
- Disciplinarians
- Nurturers
- Providers

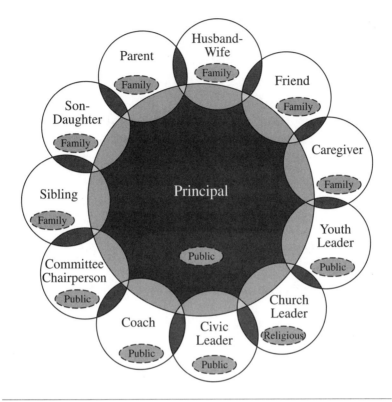

Figure 6.1   The Intersection of Family, Public, Personal, and Religious Roles

- Supporters
- Colleagues
- Collaborators
- Organizers
- Team members
- Mediators
- Health care providers
- Spokespersons

- Companions
- Role models
- Rule makers
- Umpires
- Memory keepers
- Historians
- Guardians of artifacts

The principal in this scenario should identify the roles he occupies and assess the demands and expectations that accompany each role. Using this information, he should establish the priority for each role. Some roles may need to be temporarily suspended in deference to more pressing roles. A schedule should be established so that the responsibilities of these roles can be met. Only through self-examination and planning can the principal unravel and prioritize the complexities of his professional and personal life. Through this process, he should be able to find greater satisfaction with what he accomplishes on a daily basis.

Mistake 17
Ignoring Health Issues

The sedentary work of a principal may contribute to health risks. Changes in levels of physical activity and subtle stress may gradually erode good health. Many principals make physical fitness a top priority.

Scenario 46: Good Health

Principals described neglecting their bodies or "letting their bodies go." They remembered being physically fit and exercising when they were younger and missing that aspect of their lives. Their mistake was not making their health the top issue on their "to do" lists.

Rx: The aging process and a sedentary job can cause physical decline. Regular exercise has to be planned or it will not occur. Every principal should identify the amount of physical activity necessary to maintain physical fitness. Most principals need to increase their activity levels. Increased physical activity will lead to improved physical health and mental well being. Time spent in physical activities will have an immediate positive effect on a principal's job performance. Increased activity leads to more energy, less stress, and a higher attention level. Living a healthier life will benefit the principal both personally and professionally (Brock & Grady, 2002).

Krajewski, Martin, and Walden (1983) created an ulcer-producer list. The following items from the list may contribute to a principal's health concerns:

- Work long hours
- Don't get enough rest
- Refuse to delegate
- Don't plan or manage time
- Don't establish priorities
- Don't ask others for help
- Ignore your family
- Never say no
- Always have an open door
- Try to be all things to all people
- Don't take up hobbies or sports
- Associate only with people at work
- Be a perfectionist

A principal who is concerned about health risks should consider ways to address the items on the ulcer-producer list.

Principals need to be attentive to the messages given to them by spouses, colleagues, secretaries, and friends. Close, trusted friends may be able to assist principals to recognize their diminished capacity on the job. Regularly scheduled breaks and planned vacations help to reduce the stress of work (Brock & Grady, 2002). The principal has to plan for self-renewal because the job is certain to tax the energy of even the most exuberant individual.

Schools that are well organized can function effectively and efficiently without the constant involvement of the principal. Systems and procedures should be established so that the school functions smoothly. If the principal has built trusting relationships in the school, then it is possible to delegate tasks that do not require the principal's direct involvement. By delegating tasks, the principal will have more time for attending to personal health and fitness issues.

Rooney (2000) offers the following advice:

Take care of yourself physically, emotionally, professionally, and spiritually. Enter a time in your planner for exercise or other activities you enjoy. Keep this time as sacred
as any appointment or meeting. "No, I am busy then"
covers your aerobic class as well as a scheduled staff
meeting. Spend time reflecting on your leadership. You
lead from within your own person, so nurture that
person. (p. 78)

Scenario 47: Health Risk

*A woman had been principal for 12 years. Then she got an offer to
be the principal at a newer and larger school. She took the position.
The problem was the new school was much different from the old
school. The families had more money, more education, and more
time. Eventually, the principal left the job because it was affecting
her health. She never took another principal's job.*

Rχ: Beware of the Midas Touch! Increased school size, prestige, and salary may not be a blessing. The principalship is a
demanding and inherently stressful position. Before changing
jobs or accepting a job, carefully consider what the demands
and challenges of the new job might be. Destroying one's
health is the ultimate negative consequence of a misguided
career decision.

Find out what happened to the previous principal at the
school before accepting a position. There may have been a
series of principals who moved through the principalship of
the school, signaling a long-standing difficulty. Did the principal retire or was the principal encouraged to leave? Did the
principal leave the job because there were too many troubling
aspects to it? Without this information, it would be unwise to
accept the position.

Occasionally a school will have long-standing difficulties.
These difficulties may be the result of family feuds or parent

groups who seek to impose their agenda on the school. When these situations exist, it may require careful planning for a principal to succeed when confronting a history of local conflict.

Understanding the history of a school, the community, and the tenure of previous principals should be part of the research an individual completes before accepting a position. Asking questions, visiting the community, reading old newspapers, and visiting with the area principals are ways to learn the history of a school.

Aristotle's dictum, "know thyself" is particularly applicable in this scenario. Individuals who have been successful at one school may fail to recognize the conditions of the job and the personal skills that made them successful. Those same conditions may not exist in the new school. Different skills may be needed. Rushing to a "new rung" on the career ladder without assessing one's skills and determining the fit with the new job can be disastrous.

Accepting a new position is a significant life event for an adult. The work invested in preparation for a change is time well spent.

Mistake 18
Succumbing to Stress

Stress is invisible and insidious. Skilled principals structure their work and their days to reduce the incidence of stress.

Scenario 48: Anger Alert

> *Teachers reported their reluctance to take their concerns to the principal. They said she just does not have any patience. She seems to be angry all the time. When they try to talk to her, she just explodes. These sudden outbursts are unpredictable.*

Rχ: Principals need to collect information about their behavior and actions. The best situation is for a principal to have someone who can alert her when her anger or stress is showing. If this is impossible, then the principal should distribute a survey designed to answer the question "How am I doing?"

Peurifoy (1999) provided the following key ideas concerning anger:

1. Anger is an automatic, emotional response to a real or perceived threat. It generates energy as well as motivation to eliminate the threat. The greater the threat, the higher the level of arousal and the greater the motivation to eliminate the threat.

2. While anger is often a destructive force, it can also enable a person to set limits and say no to unreasonable demands, and take steps to meet important needs that have been ignored.

3. A threat that triggers anger may be either real or perceived. Our responses to threats are learned. New responses can be learned to replace the old ones. (p. 5)

The result of constant stress is illness. Principals should visit their physicians regularly to keep the effects of stress under control. The principal in this scenario would benefit from discussing her anger and impatience with a medical professional.

Stress reducers have to be part of the principal's arsenal as well. Whether this is time in the gym, walking, aerobic classes, or other physical activity, these outlets need to be used daily. Physical activities reduce stress. School issues should be resolved outside the home and away from the family.

Establishing a network with other principals can help to reduce the anxiety, frustration, and stress related to the principalship. Regular meetings with colleagues can help to reduce the isolation of the principalship. School issues can be discussed during these meetings, and families can be relieved of the burden of listening to "tales from the job."

Time alone is essential. Quiet time provides an opportunity for reflection and renewal. Privacy affords an opportunity to get emotions under control.

Scenario 49: Increasing Expectations

The principal described her dilemma. She said she is expected to meet the state standards for student performance, yet the conditions of the school faculty, staff, and students make the expectation unrealistic. She said she is constantly troubled by this situation.

Rχ: This principal is describing job stress. She is in a position where the expectations and demands of the job are creating tension.

Many principals must confront the stress that accompanies the increased expectations for student performance. Achieving these high expectations requires that teachers and staff members be committed to meeting these standards. Teacher and staff skills must be adequate to the task.

For the principal, this means that new teachers must have the skills to help students meet the performance standards. All teachers must be provided with the professional development opportunities they need to help students reach the performance standards. The principal must secure the resources to provide these opportunities for teachers. To accomplish this, the principal must be skilled at working with central office administrators to secure resources.

The principal must work with the students' families to communicate the expectations for student performance. Without family support, students may not be motivated to do the work required of them.

The principal must have accurate information about student performance, and be able to use this information to plan the work that must be accomplished by the students and teachers in the school. Keeping the focus on what must be accomplished is essential. The goals must be clear to all—students, teachers, staff, and families.

Job expectations are one source of stress for principals. In this scenario, the expectation is an "is." The expectation must be met. It is not a discretionary issue. The principal must establish a plan for meeting the expectation and build ownership throughout the school to achieve the goals.

There are many sources of job stress for principals. Whan and Thomas (1996) suggest the following sources:

- Finding substitutes for teacher absences
- Staff meetings, particularly when a controversial issue is raised or expected
- Working with parent groups, especially when parents are uncooperative
- Implementing government mandates or policies
- Problems with shortages, deliveries, and equipment
- School break-ins, thefts, and vandalism
- Work overload
- Time constraints
- Extracurricular duties (student activities outside of school hours)
- Meetings outside of school hours
- Working in isolation
- Lack of resources for a task
- Lack of appreciation
- Lack of control in decisions

The principal must learn to manage stress because the sources of job stress are extensive. The strategies a principal should use include the following:

- Taking care of themselves
- Engaging in activities with family and friends
- Having and following an educational philosophy
- Having a clear understanding of their role
- Networking with colleagues

- Matching their leadership style to the needs of the school
- Learning not to wallow in worry
- Laughing and encouraging laughter at work
- Approaching conflicts as problems to be solved
- Focusing on issues they can control
- Knowing how to manage their time
- Having excellent interpersonal skills (Brock & Grady, 2002, p. 63)

Mistake 19
Etiquette Gaffes

The principal represents the school and holds an important and highly visible position in the community. All eyes are on the principal, and appearances do matter.

Scenario 50: The Clothes Make the Man and the Woman

The teachers described their irritation about the way the principal dressed. They acknowledged that clothes were not supposed to be important, but their principal was always "poorly put together." His pants were always wrinkled and did not fit him. He would wear shirts and ties that did not match. When he did not wear a tie, he wore a worn-out polo shirt that could be worn to cut the lawn. He was not particularly clean either. His hands were grimy, and if he bothered to shave, he did a haphazard job. They expected the principal to look neat and clean.

Rχ: The principalship is a position of public trust and confidence. Based on the description of this principal's appearance, he does not inspire trust or confidence. Individuals are judged on appearances. A principal's knowledge of teaching and learning may be totally discounted simply because he is not professionally attired.

The principal and teachers are role models for the students. A slovenly presentation does not provide a good role model for students. Parents and the public expect more. The principal needs to reconsider the importance of a professional appearance and adjust his hygiene and attire accordingly.

> Most of us dislike the implications of the old axiom that clothes make the man; yet we know it contains more than a grain of truth . . . where clothes make the woman as well . . . when there are two equally qualified candidates for a new position, the one who "looks the part" is chosen over the one whose appearance is less so . . . keep in mind that an employee represents not him—or herself, but the [school] he or she works for. (Post, 1997, p. 99)

No school wants its image to be unprofessional.

Principal evaluations provide a means for gathering information about a principal's performance. This principal would benefit from using an evaluation tool to gather information about himself.

> Whether intentionally or not, principals send messages by the way they are dressed and groomed. Clothing reflects the personality, attitudes, and values of the wearer. Dress can either alienate or persuade. Appropriate dress is a method of expressing respect for both the particular situation and the people in it. (Miller, 1988, pp. 18–19)

Scenario 51: Talk Less, Hear More

> *The teacher was irate as she related her experience. She said, "At the end of a school day, I was visiting with one of my 'problem' students about his late assignments and reminding him about the deal we had. The principal walked in, and not knowing what we were talking about, she said one thing to this student and the student just exploded. The principal ended up marching him to her office for an hour of after school detention."*

Rχ: "Don't interrupt others" is a common rule of courtesy that should be learned as a child. This principal's interference precipitated a problem for the student and the teacher.

Experienced principals know that if a teacher needs assistance, the teacher will call. In this instance, the principal should have waited outside the room until the teacher was finished with the student interaction.

There is no way to know the background of this teacher's interactions with the student. The teacher may have spent a very long time building rapport with the student. All of the teacher's careful work with the student could be destroyed by one rude interruption.

The teacher's description suggests that the principal was simply meddling. Principals need to understand a situation before becoming involved in teacher-student interactions. This principal may, in fact, have punished the student for responding to the principal's own rude intrusion.

Nearly all the faults or mistakes commonly made in conversation are caused by not thinking or by lack of consideration . . . Many of us do not have anyone to remind us about our thoughtless and inconsiderate talk. Only by careful listening to our own words and strict attention to the reactions of our listeners can we discover our personal inadequacies. The burden of thinking before speaking is our own. Dorothy Sarnoff wrote: "'I' is the smallest letter in the alphabet. Don't make it the largest word in your vocabulary. Say, with Socrates, not "I think," but "What do you think?" (Post, 1997, p. 4)

VII

Fatal Attractions

Leave all hope, ye that enter.

Dante Alighieri
Divine Comedy (c. 1300)
Inferno, Canto III, Line 9

O ne individual suggested that mistakes that involve moral issues should not be included in a book about the mistakes principals make. Certainly the message of this section is

> Stop!
> Do Not Do the Following!

The unfortunate reality is that occasionally principals do make career-ending mistakes. These are the worst mistakes because they cause the most damage to the principals, schools, students, and communities.

These types of mistakes make headlines in the newspapers. In many cases, the only suggestions that can be offered are "don't do that!" or "pick another career." There is no happy ending to these mistakes—but they do reflect a small number of individuals in the principal's role.

Mistake 20
Errors of Judgment

The mistakes that reflect errors of judgment include becoming personally involved with students, driving under the influence of alcohol, inappropriate conduct in public, and taking school property. The public expectation is that principals should never make mistakes such as these. Unfortunately, occasionally mistakes of this type are made.

Scenario 52: Leave the Girls Alone

A high school principal lost his job. He had been principal for nine years. Before being named principal he coached basketball and football. He was only 37. His mistake was getting involved with some of the high school girls. No one could believe he would do this. He was married and had kids of his own in the school. Everyone was very upset by this.

Rχ: Getting personally involved with students is an obvious mistake. The principal is responsible for ensuring the safety of the students (Grady, 1995; Grady et al., 1996). This principal's mistake has potential legal and professional ramifications.

Whether unwanted advances are made by principals, teachers, or students, the behavior cannot be tolerated. Reports of cases of harassment include principals and teachers who prey on students and teachers, as well as students who harass other students. According to a report in the *Detroit Free Press*

(1993), results of a survey of 1,632 eighth through eleventh graders indicate that "85 percent of girls and 76 percent of boys report they have been sexually harassed" (p. 6A).

The abuse that occurs in schools can be verbal or physical. False accusations are always a possibility. Professional reputations can be destroyed by false accusations. However, Shakeshaft and Cohan (1995) investigated 335 cases of students who reported sexual abuse by teachers or professional staff and found that only 7.5% of the accusations were false.

The principal's task is to ensure that harassment policies and procedures are in place, are understood by all school personnel, and are followed. Most importantly, the principal must be a model of virtue.

Scenario 53: Watch Out for That Car!

A principal left a meeting late one evening. Apparently he had had too much to drink. He sideswiped four cars on his way home. Someone reported his license number to the police and he was arrested.

Another high school principal was arrested for DUI—on a school night! The principal was 43. The community reported that they invested tremendous effort trying to teach the kids about the dangers of alcohol and other drugs. They raised questions about the type of role model the principal was.

Rχ: The message the principals needed was "Don't drink and drive." Individuals with drinking problems need to get assistance. The principalship requires individuals who exercise good judgment. These principals' lack of good judgment was apparent. The principalship is a position of public trust. Behavior such as this does not inspire trust.

The principal is the leader of the school, and the principal's job does not end at 5:00 P.M. No matter where the principal goes or what the principal does, that individual is always the principal of the school. The principal is expected to display the highest standards of behavior. Community members, parents, students, and teachers will rarely tolerate the behavior described in these scenarios. The role is too public, and the expectations that the principal will be a positive role model are clear.

Considerable emphasis is placed on permeating schools with a "Drug Free" message. Constant national campaigns are designed to reach the student populations in the U.S. with the message about the negative effects of alcohol and drugs. As the leader of a school, and the purveyor of the anti-alcohol, anti-drug message, the principal has to be the model of the message for the students and faculty.

Scenario 54: Not on the Clock

A high school principal was arrested for lewd conduct. Apparently he invited an undercover agent into his car and proceeded to grope him. This happened in a local park.

Another principal was arrested in a local park. He was in a school district car. Apparently he and the woman he was with had their clothes off and were having a good time. It was the middle of the day. The woman was not his wife.

Rχ: Mistakes such as these may be fatal to a principal's career. The principal is expected to be a model citizen. The public is clear in its demands that the principal be a positive role model for the students. Only in a rare situation could a principal expect to "survive" this type of mistake.

The principalship is a twenty-four hour, seven day a week job. No matter where the principal goes, the principal is the principal. The role provides little privacy; public scrutiny is constant. An individual who accepts a principal's position must be willing to meet the public's expectations for scrupulous behavior.

Remember these rules: When driving the school district vehicle never break *any* laws. Keep your clothes on, do not violate traffic laws, do not park the vehicle in a questionable location, use the vehicle for school business only. Always use good judgment.

The principal is expected to be a paragon of virtue—a model for students and teachers. These principals did not exercise good judgment. Fortunately, very few principals make these mistakes.

Scenario 55: Mistaken Ownership

A principal took three new trees that were supposed to be planted around the school. He planted them around his house instead. He lost his job because of this.

In another high school, there was a drawer for money from outside rentals of the gym and pop sales. The money disappeared. The principal was accused of stealing it. He lost his job. Later it was determined that it was actually his wife who took the cash.

Rχ: Stealing school property appears to be a certain path to termination. As a public servant, a principal's behavior must always be above reproach. The basic principles of "do not steal, do not lie" must be fundamental to a principal's code of behavior.

The illusion of power in the principalship and the belief that "power corrupts" may be reflected in these principals' choices. The number one quality employees want in a leader is integrity—integrity in all things, big and small (Kouzes & Posner, 2002). The principal is responsible for the safe-keeping of school funds. Although most principals do not have access to "big" money, any amount of money can be a threat to a principal's job if mishandled. Keeping money in drawers at school is not a safe money management practice. Cash poses a clear temptation. Loose change and loose management need to be eliminated. Money handling procedures must be in place, as well as a system that ensures that no one person receives or spends money independently.

Money that may funnel through a principal's office includes class fees; athletic revenues; concert, play, and program receipts; school sales; and possibly PTA and booster funds. It is often common practice to maintain a small cash reserve in the office to make change or purchase small items. The principal must account for these funds. If any improprieties occur, the principal will be held responsible for them.

The Leader's Response

Response 1
Never to Err Again?

Interestingly, the goal of the leader is not to be free of mistakes, or to fear making mistakes, but to avoid making the same mistake a second time. Conrad Hilton, a hotel executive, said "Success seems to be connected with action. Successful people keep moving. They make mistakes, but they don't quit" (Maxwell, 1999, p. 66).

Maxwell (1999) framed the qualities of leaders with the following question:

What qualities do leaders possess that enable them to make things happen?

1. They know what they want . . .

2. They push themselves to act . . .

3. They take more risks . . .

4. They make more mistakes. (pp. 69–70)

The good news for initiators is that they make things happen. The bad news is that they make lots of mistakes. IBM founder Thomas J. Watson recognized that when he remarked, "The way to succeed is to double your failure rate."

Even though initiators experience more failures, they do not let this bother them. The greater the potential, the greater the chance for failure. Senator Robert Kennedy summed it up: "Only those who dare to fail greatly can ever achieve greatly." If you want to achieve great things as a leader, you must be willing to initiate and put yourself on the line (Maxwell, 1999).

The principal cannot be immobilized by the fear of risk taking or of making mistakes. In fact, the leader is distinguished by a willingness to take risks (Grady & LeSourd, 1990). Instead, the principal must be attentive to gathering adequate information, soliciting the perspectives of all who should be involved in a decision, and acting decisively using all relevant data to make decisions. The principal must be conscious of past mistakes and the mistakes of other principals and schools so that these mistakes are not repeated.

"We are the sum total of all the choices we have made. There is scarcely an hour of the day in which we are not called upon to make choices of one sort or another, trivial or far reaching" (Roosevelt, 1960, p. 160–161).

It is by making choices that principals avoid repeating the mistakes of the past.

Response 2
Over the Horizon

The future of the principalship will continue to be marked by the challenges of change. Tirozzi (2001) enumerated emerging issues such as high-stakes testing, demands for new teachers, questions of resource allocation, and technology concerns. Legislative mandates will shape the direction of public education as each wave of political leaders attempts to influence the work and outcomes of public schools. Even as new issues take prominence in the schools, principals must continue to exercise skill in interpersonal relations—human relations, working with professionals and parents, being the best principal leader, managing the endless work and time constraints of the job, handling the complex tasks of the principalship, being guardians of their personal lives, and avoiding career-ending fatal mistakes. The principalship demands individuals who are intelligent, reflective, future oriented, resilient, and experienced.

Chapko and Buchko (2001) offered the following tips for surviving in the principalship:

- Maintain a sense of humor
- Grow thicker skin to deflect the negative comments that will be hurled at you
- Try not to take the negative stuff personally
- Realize that it is impossible to please everyone, no matter how hard you try
- Regard parents as your greatest potential allies
- Work as a team with your entire staff
- Value and respect the individual strengths of each staff member
- Hire the best teachers available
- Take time to enjoy your students
- Above all, always make decisions based on what's best for your students (p. 39)

The principalship has many rewards that are counted in the success of students and teachers. Through the principal's leadership, lives are transformed. By avoiding the mistakes of others, principals create positive, successful school environments.

Resource A

Building Visibility in the Community

A s principal, am I using these opportunities to be known and visible to the community?

Opportunity	Yes	No
Community meetings		
Parent-teacher meetings		
Carnivals		
Open house		
Newsletters		
E-mail		
Web site		
Newspaper		
Television		
Radio		
Extracurricular activities		
Baseball		
Basketball		
Football		
Soccer		
Tennis		
Volleyball		
Plays		
Concerts		
Debate		
Club activities		

Resource B

Verbal Skills Self-Assessment

Indicate with a check mark (✓) whether you display each of these skills.

My Verbal Skills	Yes	No*
1. I communicate my ideas clearly and effectively.		
2. I have excellent English skills.		
3. I recognize and respond to verbal and nonverbal cues.		
4. I avoid "fad" language.		
5. I refrain from dominating conversations.		
6. I am attentive to the different needs of different audiences.		
7. I am knowledgeable about cultural differences.		
8. I am known for having a positive word for everyone I meet.		

*Make an improvement plan for these skills.

Resource C

Principal Access Self-Assessment

Following are self-assessment questions about your accessibility as a principal. After you respond to each question, suggest your goal for improvement in that area.

	Yes	*No*
• Do I distribute a weekly schedule of my activities?		
Goal for Improvement:		
• Are my out-of-building activities detracting from my building responsibilities?		
Goal for Improvement:		
• Does the secretary know my schedule?		
Goal for Improvement:		

	Yes	No
• When individuals inquire about me, does the secretary let them know when I will be available?		
Goal for Improvement:		
• Do I vary my schedule so that teachers have access to me?		
Goal for Improvement:		
• Do I greet the teachers and staff daily?		
Goal for Improvement:		

Resource D

Principal Self-Assessment

Identify your strengths and weaknesses by responding to each of the following items.

Do I	Yes	No	Don't Know
Listen			
Look for strengths			
Resolve conflicts promptly			
Respond to questions			
Behave as a positive role model			
Seek others' perspectives			
Build collaboration			
Conduct regular teacher evaluations			
Maintain a professional work environment			
Avoid favoritism			
Provide information			
Take responsibility for delivering "bad" news			

	Yes	No	Don't Know
Greet everyone			
Give consistent messages			
Provide opportunities for individual visits			
Acknowledge the expertise of others			
Recognize the importance of informal groups			
Work with all teachers			
Respond to parents			
Treat adults as adults			
Consider the impact of proposed changes			
Note accomplishments			
Make timely decisions			
Use time effectively			
Provide professional development opportunities			
Exercise good judgment			

References

Autry, J. A. (2001). *The servant leader: How to build a creative team, develop great morale, and improve bottom-line performance.* Roseville, CA: Prima.

Barth, R. S. (1990). *Improving schools from within.* San Francisco: Jossey-Bass.

Beck, L. G., & Murphy, J. (1993). *Understanding the principalship.* New York: Teachers College Press.

Bennis, W., & Nanus, B. (1997). *Leaders: The strategies for taking charge* (2nd ed.). New York: Harper and Row.

Bergman, A. B. (1992). Lessons for principals from site-based management. *Educational Leadership, 50*(1), 48–51.

Blanchard, K., & Johnson, S. (1983). *The one minute manager.* New York: Berkley Books.

Blanchard, K., & McBride, M. (2003). *The one minute apology: A powerful way to make things better.* New York: William Morrow.

Blase, J., & Blase, J. (2002). The dark side of leadership: Teacher perspectives of principal mistreatment. *Educational Administration Quarterly, 38*(5), 671–727.

Blase, J., & Kirby, P. C. (2000). *Bringing out the best in teachers: What effective principals do* (2nd ed.). Thousand Oaks, CA: Corwin Press.

Blumberg, A. (1986). *The language of supervision: Perspectives over time.* Paper presented at the annual meeting of the American Educational Research Association, San Francisco, CA. April 16–20. (ERIC Document Reproduction Service No. ED277110)

Bolman, L. G., & Deal, T. E. (1995). *Leading with soul: An uncommon journey of spirit.* San Francisco: Jossey-Bass.

Brock, B. L., & Grady, M. L. (2000). *Rekindling the flame: Principals combating teacher burnout.* Thousand Oaks, CA: Corwin Press.

Brock, B. L., & Grady, M. L. (2001). *From first-year to first rate: Principals guiding beginning teachers* (2nd ed.). Thousand Oaks, CA: Corwin Press.

Brock, B. L., & Grady, M. L. (2002). *Avoiding burnout: A principal's guide to keeping the fire alive.* Thousand Oaks, CA: Corwin Press.

Bulach, C., Boothe, D., & Pickett, W. (1998). "Should nots" for school principals: Teachers share their views. *ERS Spectrum, 16*(1), 16–20.

Bulach, C., Pickett, W., & Boothe, D. (1998). *Mistakes educational leaders make.* ERIC Digest 122. (ERIC Document Reproduction Service No. ED422604)

Caine, R. N., & Caine, G. (1991). *Making connections: Teaching and the human brain.* Alexandria, VA: Association for Supervision and Curriculum Development.

Caine, R. N., & Caine, G. (1997). *Education on the edge of possibility.* Alexandria, VA: Association for Supervision and Curriculum Development.

Carlson, R. O. (1962). *Executive succession and organizational change.* Chicago: University of Chicago Midwest Administrator Center.

Carter, J. (1996). *Living faith.* New York: Random House.

Chapko, M. A., & Buchko, M. (2001). Surviving the principalship. *Principal, 74*(2), 38–39.

Charan, R. (2002). Conquering a culture of indecision. In *Harvard Business Review on Culture and Change* (pp. 143–164). Boston: Harvard Business School.

Cohn, K. C. (1989, November). *Factors associated with the involuntary reassessment of three women principals.* Paper presented at the annual meeting of the American Educational Research Association on Research on Women and Education, San Diego, CA.

Conradt, C. (2001). The whale story. In J. Canfield, M. V. Hansen, M. Rogerson, M. Rutte, & T. Clauss, *Chicken soup for the soul at work: 101 stories of courage, compassion and creativity in the workplace* (pp. 91–93). Deerfield Beach, FL: Health Communications.

Damasio, A. R. (1994). *Descartes' error.* New York: Avon.

Davis, S. (1998). Why do principals get fired? *Principal, 78*(2), 34–39.

Davis, S. (2000). Why principals lose their jobs: Comparing the perceptions of principals and superintendents. *Journal of School Leadership, 10*(1), 40–68.

Deal, T. E., & Kennedy, A. A. (1982). *Corporate cultures: The rites and rituals of corporate life.* Reading, MA: Addison-Wesley.

Detroit Free Press. (1993, June 2). p. 6A.

Drake, T. L., & Roe, W. H. (2003). *The principalship* (6th ed.). Upper Saddle River, NJ: Merrill Prentice Hall.

Driscoll, M., & Kerchner, C. (1999). The implications of social capital for schools, communities, and cities: Educational administration as if a sense of place mattered. In J. Murphy and K. Louis (Eds.), *Handbook of research on educational administration* (p. 373–396). San Francisco: Jossey-Bass.

Duggan, M. A. (1997). *Powerful parent letters for K–3.* Thousand Oaks, CA: Corwin Press.

Elias, M. J., Zins, J. E., Weissberg, R. P., Frey, K. S., Greenberg, M. T., Haynes, N. M., et al. (1997). *Promoting social and emotional learning*. Alexandria, VA: Association for Supervision and Curriculum Development.

Enoch, S. W. (1995). The dynamics of home-school relationships. *The School Administrator, 52*(10), 24–26.

Eskelin, N. (2001). *Leading with love . . . and getting more results*. Grand Rapids, MI: Fleming H. Revell.

Fagan, J. (2001). There's no place like school. *Principal, 80*(5), 36–37.

Finkelstein, S. (2003, July). 7 habits of spectacularly unsuccessful executives. *Fast Company*, 84–89.

Freedman, S. G. (1990). *Small victories: The real world of a teacher, her students, and their high school*. New York: Harper Perennial.

Fullan, M. G. (1988). *What's worth fighting for in the principalship? Strategies for taking charge in the elementary school principalship*. Toronto: Ontario Public School Teachers' Federation.

Fullan, M. G. (2001). *Leading in a culture of change*. San Francisco: Jossey-Bass.

Giba, M. A. (1998). Empowering teachers to lead: How far should a principal go in providing leadership opportunities for teachers? *Principal, 78*(1), 49–53.

Giles, H. C. (1998). *Parent engagement as a school reform strategy*. ERIC Clearinghouse on Urban Education. (ERIC Document Reproduction Service No. ED032215)

Glickman, C. D. (2003). *SuperVision and instructional leadership: A developmental approach*. New York: Allyn & Bacon.

Grady, M. L. (1990). The teaching principal. *Research in Rural Education, 6*(3), 49–52.

Grady, M. L. (1995). Creating safe schools: Policies and practices. In K. Lane, M. Richardson, & D. Van Berkum (Eds.), *Safe schools: What are they? How can I create one?* (pp. 137–160). Lancaster, PA: Technomic Press.

Grady, M. L. (2000). The torrid tale of a superintendent's secretary. *The School Administrator, 57*(6), 41.

Grady, M. L., Bendezú, M. A., & Brock, B. L. (1996). Principals' perceptions of school safety. *Leadership Nebraska, 6*, 18–20.

Grady, M. L., & LeSourd, S. (1990). Principals' attitudes toward visionary leadership. *The High School Journal, 73*(2), 103–110.

Grady, M. L., Wayson, W. W., & Zirkel, P. A. (1989). A review of effective schools research as it relates to effective principals. In F. C. Wendel & M. T. Bryant (Eds.), *UCEA Monograph Series* (pp. 5–33). Tempe, AZ: UCEA.

Greenspan, S. I. (1997). *The growth of the mind*. Reading, MA: Addison-Wesley.

Haar, J. (2001a, October). Improving school quality through principal professional development. *Joint Center for the Study of the Superintendency,* 2–3.

Haar, J. (2001b). Professional development for principals. *Journal of the Northern Interior Staff Development Council, 6*(2), 2–3.

Haar, J. (2001c, October 24–26). *Providing professional development for rural educators.* Paper presented at the Annual Meeting of the National Rural Education Association, Albuquerque, NM.

Haar, J. (2002a, March 1–2). *Leadership and school culture.* Paper presented at the Annual Meeting of the International Academy of Educational Leaders, Atlanta, GA.

Haar, J. (2002b). *A multiple case study: Principals' involvement in professional development.* Unpublished Dissertation, University of Nebraska.

Hanson, E. M. (2003). *Educational Administration and Organizational Behavior* (5th ed.). Boston: Pearson Education.

Haye, J. (2001). It takes Chutzpah! In J. Canfield, M. V. Hansen, M. Rogerson, M. Rutte, & T. Clauss, *Chicken soup for the soul at work: 101 stories of courage, compassion and creativity in the workplace* (pp. 338–340). Deerfield, FL: Health Communications.

Heleen, O. (1992). Is your school family-friendly? *Principal, 72*(2), 5–8.

Hines, R. W. (1993). Principal starts with PR. *Principal, 72*(3), 45–46.

Hoy, W. K., & Miskel, C. G. (2000). *Educational administration: Theory, research, and practice.* New York: McGraw-Hill.

Irmsher, K. (1996). *Communication Skills.* ERIC Digest, Clearinghouse on Educational Management, University of Oregon. (ERIC Document No. EA027190)

Jensen, E. (1998). *Teaching with the brain in mind.* Alexandria, VA: Association for Supervision and Curriculum Development.

Kouzes, J. M., & Posner, B. Z. (2002). *The leadership challenge: How to keep getting extraordinary things done in organizations* (3rd ed.). San Francisco: Jossey-Bass.

Krajewski, R. J., Martin, J. S., & Walden, J. C. (1983). *The elementary school principalship.* New York: Holt, Rinehart and Winston.

Krupp, J. A. (1994). Motivation begins with you. *Principal, 74*(2), 27–29.

LeBoeuf, M. (1985). *The greatest management principle in the world.* New York: G. P. Putnam's Sons.

LeDoux, J. (1996). *The emotional brain.* New York: Simon & Schuster.

Lyman, L. L. (2000). *How do they know you care? The principal's challenge.* New York: Teachers College Press.

Maggio, R. (1990). *How to say it: Choice words, phrases, sentences, and paragraphs for every situation.* Paramus, NJ: Prentice Hall.

Marriott, D. (2001). Managing school culture. *Principal, 81*(1), 75–77.

Martin-Lucchesi, J. (1990). *Superintendents and unsuccessful principals: A study in Washington State.* Unpublished doctoral dissertation, Washington State University, Pullman.

Maslow, A. H. (1998). *Maslow on management.* New York: John Wiley & Sons.

Maxwell, J. C. (1999). *The 21 indispensable qualities of a leader: Becoming the person others will want to follow.* Nashville, TN: Thomas Nelson.

Miller, P. W. (1988). *Nonverbal communication* (3rd ed.). Washington, DC: National Education Association.

Mintzberg, H., Jorgensen, J., Dougherty, D., & Westley, F. (1996). Some surprising things about collaboration—Knowing how people connect makes it better. *Organizational Dynamics, 25*(1), 60–71.

Peurifoy, R. Z. (1999). *Anger: Taming the beast.* New York: Kodansha International.

Pierce, P. R. (1935). *The origin and development of the public school principalship.* Chicago: The University of Chicago Libraries.

Post, P. (1997). *Emily Post's etiquette* (16th ed.). New York: Harper-Collins.

Richards, L. N., & Schmiege, C. J. (1993). Problems and strengths of single-parent families: Implications for practice and policy. *Family Relations, 42,* 277–285.

Rogers, E. M. (1995). *Diffusion of innovations* (4th ed.). New York: The Free Press.

Rooney, J. (2000). Survival skills for the new principal. *Educational Leadership, 58*(1), 77–78.

Roosevelt, E. (1960). *You learn by living.* New York: Harper.

Sergiovanni, T. J. (1994). *Building community in schools.* San Francisco: Jossey-Bass.

Shakeshaft, C., & Cohan, A. (1995, March). Sexual abuse of students by school personnel. *Phi Delta Kappan, 76,* 512–520.

Skelly, K. (1996). A letter to a newly appointed principal: Ten tips for making the grade. *Bulletin, 80*(577), 90–96.

Sylwester, R. (1995). *A celebration of neurons: An educator's guide to the human brain.* Alexandria, VA: Association for Supervision and Curriculum Development.

Tatum, J. B. (1995). Meditations on servant-leadership. In L. C. Spears (Ed.), *Reflections on leadership: How Robert K. Greenleaf's theory of servant-leadership influenced today's top management thinkers* (pp. 308–312). New York: John Wiley & Sons.

Tirozzi, G. N. (2001). The artistry of leadership: The evoking role of the secondary school principal. *Phi Delta Kappan, 82*(6), 434–439.

Tooms, A. (2003). The rookie's playbook: Insights and dirt for new principals. *Phi Delta Kappan, 530–533.*

Vienne, V. (1998). *The art of doing nothing: Simple ways to make time for yourself.* New York: Clarkson Potter.

Watkins, P. (1993). Five strategies for managing angry parents. *Principal, 72*(4), 29–30.

Weber, F. N., III. (1995). The principal as mirror-maker. *Momentum, 26*(3), 69–71.

Weller, L. J., Jr., & Weller, S. (2000). *Quality human resources leadership: A principal's handbook.* Lanham, MD: Scarecrow.

Whan, L. D., & Thomas, A. R. (1996). The principalship and stress in the workplace: An observational and physiological study. *Journal of School Leadership, 6*(4), 444–465.

Wheatley, M. J. (1993). *Leadership and the new science: Learning about organization from an orderly universe.* San Francisco: Barrett-Koehler.

Whitaker, B. (1997). Instructional leadership and principal visibility. *The Clearinghouse, 70*(3), 155–156.

Wilkins, A. L. (1989). *Developing corporate character: How to successfully change an organization without destroying it.* San Francisco: Jossey-Bass.

Wills, G. (1994). *Certain trumpets: The call of leaders.* New York: Simon & Schuster.

Zalman, C. C., & Bryant, M. T. (2002, April). *The Solomonic pathway: Critical incidents in the elementary school principalship.* Paper presented at the annual meeting of the American Educational Research Association, New Orleans, LA.

**CORWIN
PRESS**

The Corwin Press logo—a raven striding across an open book—represents the union of courage and learning. Corwin Press is committed to improving education for all learners by publishing books and other professional development resources for those serving the field of K–12 education. By providing practical, hands-on materials, Corwin Press continues to carry out the promise of its motto: **"Helping Educators Do Their Work Better."**